MASSACHUSETTS HIKING

JACQUELINE TOURVILLE

How to Use This Book

ABOUT THE TRAIL PROFILES

Each hike in this book is listed in a consistent, easy-to-read format to help you choose the ideal hike. From a general overview of the setting to detailed driving directions, the profile will provide all the information you need. Here is a sample profile:

Map number and hike number →

Round-trip mileage → 9.0 mi/5.0 hrs
(unless otherwise noted) and the approximate amount of time needed to complete the hike (actual times can vary widely, especially on longer hikes)

1 SOMEWHERE USA HIKE

Difficulty and quality ratings ←

at the mouth of the Somewhere River ←

General location of the trail, named by its proximity to the nearest major town or landmark

BEST (

Each hike in this book begins with a brief overview of its setting. The description typically covers what kind of terrain to expect, what might be seen, and any conditions that may make the hike difficult to navigate. Side trips, such as to waterfalls or panoramic vistas, in addition to ways to combine the trail with others nearby for a longer outing, are also noted here. In many cases, mile-by-mile trail directions are included.

Symbol indicating that the hike is listed among the author's top picks

User Groups: This section notes the types of users that are permitted on the trail, including hikers, mountain bikers, horseback riders, and dogs. Wheelchair access is also noted here.

Permits: This section notes whether a permit is required for hiking, or, if the hike spans more than one day, whether one is required for camping. Any fees, such as for parking, day use, or entrance, are also noted here.

Maps: This section provides information on how to obtain detailed trail maps of the hike and its environs. Whenever applicable, names of U.S. Geologic Survey (USGS) topographic maps and national forest maps are also included; contact information for these and other map sources are noted in the Resources section at the back of this book.

Directions: This section provides mile-by-mile driving directions to the trailhead from the nearest major town.

Contact: This section provides an address and phone number for each hike. The contact is usually the agency maintaining the trail but may also be a trail club or other organization.

ABOUT THE ICONS

The icons in this book are designed to provide at-a-glance information on the difficulty and quality of each hike.

The **difficulty rating** (rated **1–5** with **1** being the lowest and **5** the highest) is based on the steepness of the trail and how difficult it is to traverse.

The **quality rating** (rated **1–10** with **1** being the lowest and **10** the highest) is based largely on scenic beauty, but also takes into account how crowded the trail is and whether noise of nearby civilization is audible.

ABOUT THE DIFFICULTY RATINGS

Trails rated 1 are very easy and suitable for hikers of all abilities, including young children.

Trails rated 2 are easy-to-moderate and suitable for most hikers, including families with active children 6 and older.

Trails rated 3 are moderately challenging and suitable for reasonably fit adults and older children who are very active.

Trails rated 4 are very challenging and suitable for physically fit hikers who are seeking a workout.

Trails rated 5 are extremely challenging and suitable only for experienced hikers who are in top physical condition.

MAP SYMBOLS

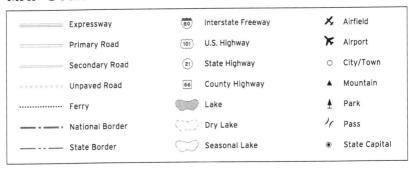

Expressway	Interstate Freeway	Airfield
Primary Road	U.S. Highway	Airport
Secondary Road	State Highway	City/Town
Unpaved Road	County Highway	Mountain
Ferry	Lake	Park
National Border	Dry Lake	Pass
State Border	Seasonal Lake	State Capital

Hiking Tips

HIKING ESSENTIALS

It doesn't require much more than a little wilderness knowledge and a backpack's worth of key items to ensure your day hike in New England is a safe and fun adventure. Here's a list of outdoor essentials.

Water and Food

Like any physical activity, hiking increases your body's fluid needs by a factor of two or more. A good rule of thumb for an all-day hike is two liters of water per person, but even that could leave you mildly dehydrated, so carry a third liter if you can. Dehydration can lead to other—more serious—problems, like heat exhaustion, hypothermia, frostbite, and injury. If you're well hydrated, you will urinate frequently and your urine will be clear. The darker your urine, the greater your level of dehydration. If you feel thirsty, dehydration has already commenced. In short: Drink a lot.

Streams and brooks run everywhere in New England. If you're out for more than a day in the backcountry, finding water is rarely a problem (except on ridge tops and summits). But microscopic organisms *Giardia lamblia* and *Cryptosporidium* are common in backcountry water sources and can cause a litany of terrible gastrointestinal problems in humans. Assume you should always treat water from backcountry sources, whether by using a filter or iodine tablets, boiling, or another proven method to eliminate giardiasis and other harmful bacteria. Day-hikers will usually find it more convenient to simply carry enough water from home for the hike.

Similarly, your body consumes a phenomenal amount of calories walking up and down a mountain. Feed it frequently. Carbohydrate-rich foods such as bread, chocolate, dried fruit, fig bars, snack bars, fresh vegetables, and energy bars are all good sources for a quick burst of energy. Fats contain about twice the calories per pound than carbs or protein, and provide the slow-burning fuel that keeps you going all day and keeps you warm through the night if you're sleeping outside; sate your need for fats by eating cheese, chocolate, canned meats or fish, pepperoni, sausage, or nuts.

On hot days, "refrigerate" your water and perishables such as cheese and chocolate: Fill a water bottle (the collapsible kind works best) with very cold water, and ice cubes if possible. Wrap it and your perishables in a thick, insulating fleece and bury it inside your pack. Or the night before, fill a water bottle halfway and freeze it, then fill the remainder with water in the morning before you leave for the hike.

Trail Maps

A map of the park, preserve, or public land you are visiting is essential. Even if you have hiked a trail a hundred times, carry a map. Unexpected trail closures, an injury requiring a shorter route, bad weather, or an animal encounter can all result in a sudden change of plans that require map assistance. Some may believe a GPS device takes the place of a map, but this isn't always true. If you get lost, a detailed trail map showing lakes, rivers, ridge lines, trail junctions, and other landmarks is still the most reliable way to get back on trail.

Many land agencies provide free paper maps at the trailhead, though be aware that some state parks and land agencies are much more vigilant about restocking than others.

GLOBAL POSITIONING SYSTEM (GPS) DEVICES

Working with a system of orbiting satellites, GPS receivers are able to accurately pinpoint your position, elevation, and time anywhere on the face of the earth. Out on the trail, GPS devices can help you navigate from point to point, indicating bearings and the distance remaining to reach your destination. It can also help should you become lost.

Despite these advances, GPS technology is not a replacement for the old standby of a compass and paper topographical map. GPS units are not yet able to provide an adequately detailed view of the surrounding landscape, batteries typically wear out in less than a day, and some landscape conditions can interfere with signal strength. Still, when used in concert with topographical maps, GPS is an extremely useful addition to your navigational toolbox.

Every hike in this book lists GPS coordinates for the hike's trailhead. Use these for better road navigation on the drive to your destination. Inputting the trailhead GPS coordinates before leaving on your hike will also help you retrace your steps if you become lost.

Check the agency's website to see if maps can be printed out beforehand or call to request a map be sent to you. For hikers along the Appalachian Trail, numerous trail maps are available. The best—and most complete—maps are published by the Appalachian Mountain Club and the Appalachian Trail Conservancy.

BLAZES AND CAIRNS

New England's forests abound with blazes—slashes of paint on trees used to mark trails. Sometimes the color of blazes seems random and unrelated to other trails in the same area, but most major trails and trail systems are blazed consistently. The Appalachian Trail (AT) bears white blazes for its entire length, including its 734 miles through five New England states. Most side trails connecting to the AT are blue-blazed. Vermont's 270-mile Long Trail, which coincides with the AT for more than 100 miles, is also blazed in white. Connecticut's Blue Trails system of hiking paths scattered across the state is, as the name suggests, marked entirely with blue blazes.

Although not all trails are well blazed, popular and well-maintained trails usually are—you'll see a colored slash of paint at frequent intervals at about eye level on tree trunks. Double slashes are sometimes used to indicate a sharp turn in the trail. Trails are blazed in both directions, so whenever you suspect you may have lost the trail, turn around to see whether you can find a blaze facing in the opposite direction; if so, you'll know you're still on the trail.

Above tree line, trails may be marked either with blazes painted on rock or with cairns, which are piles of stones constructed at regular intervals. In the rocky terrain on the upper slopes of New England's highest peaks, care may be needed to discern artificially constructed cairns from the landscape surrounding them, but the cairns in rocky areas are usually built higher and are obviously constructed by people.

Extra Clothing

At lower elevations amid the protection of trees or on a warm day, you may elect to bring no extra clothing for an hour-long outing, or no more than a light jacket for a few hours or more. The exception to this is in the Seacoast region, where hikes are more exposed to cool wind. But higher elevations, especially above tree line, get much colder than the valleys—about three degrees Fahrenheit per thousand feet—and winds can grow much stronger. Many a White Mountains hiker has departed from a valley basking in summerlike weather and reached a summit wracked by wintry winds and lying under a carpet of fresh snow, even during the summer months.

Insulating layers, a jacket that protects against wind and precipitation, a warm hat, gloves, a rain poncho, and extra socks are always a good idea to bring along when out on a long hike, especially when scaling New England's highest peaks. Look for wool blends or the new breed of high tech synthetics, fabrics that wick moisture from your skin and keep you dry. Even on a shorter trek, stowing a jacket, hat, and extra pair of socks in your backpack is always a good idea.

Flashlight

Carrying a flashlight in your pack is a must, even when your hike is planned to end well before dusk. Emergencies happen, and being stuck on the trail after dark without a flashlight only compounds the situation. Plus, if you have ever been in New England right before a thunderstorm, you know fast moving cloud cover can turn the landscape pitch dark in seconds. Micro flashlights with alloy skins, xenon bulbs, and a battery life of eight hours on two AA batteries provide ample illumination and won't add much weight to your pack. Throw in some spare batteries and an extra light—or just pack two flashlights to always be covered. A reliable, compact, and waterproof micro flashlight can typically be purchased for under $20.

Sunscreen and Sunglasses

As you climb to higher elevations, the strength of the sun's ultraviolet rays increases. Applying sunscreen or sunblock to exposed skin and wearing a baseball cap or wide-brimmed hat can easily prevent overexposure to sun. SPF strengths vary, but applying sunscreen at least a half-hour before heading out gives the lotion or spray enough time to take effect. When deciding which sunscreen to buy, look for a fragrance-free formula; strongly scented lotions and sprays may attract mosquitoes. And don't forget your sunglasses. Squinting into the sun for hours on end is not only bad for the delicate skin around your eyes, it's almost a certain way to develop a bad case of eye strain. Look for sunglasses with lenses that provide 100 percent UVA and UVB protection.

First-Aid Kit

It's wise to carry a compact and lightweight first-aid kit for emergencies in the backcountry, where an ambulance and hospital are often hours, rather than minutes, away. Prepare any first-aid kit with attention to the type of trip, the destination, and the needs of people hiking (for example, children or persons with medical conditions).

A basic first-aid kit consists of:

- aspirin or an anti-inflammatory
- 4 four-inch-by-four-inch gauze pads
- knife or scissors
- moleskin or Spenco Second Skin (for blisters)
- 1 roll of one-inch athletic tape
- 1 six-inch Ace bandage

- paper and pencil
- safety pins
- SAM splint (a versatile and lightweight splinting device available at many drug stores)
- several alcohol wipes
- several one-inch adhesive bandages
- tube of povidone iodine ointment (for wound care)
- 2 large handkerchiefs
- 2 large gauze pads

Pack everything into a thick, clear plastic resealable bag. And remember, merely carrying a first-aid kit does not make you safe; knowing how to use what's in it does.

HIKING GEAR

Much could be written about how to outfit oneself for hiking in a region like New England, with its significant range of elevations and latitudes, alpine zones, huge seasonal temperature swings, and fairly wet climate.

Don't leave your clothing, gear, and other equipment choices to chance. New England is packed with plenty of friendly, locally owned stores that offer quality, outdoor clothing and footwear options (and knowledgeable staff to help you). Or, take part in the venerable Yankee tradition of the swap meet. Many of New England's mountain clubs hold semi-annual or seasonal meets, giving hikers the irresistible chance to scoop up quality used gear at a very frugal price. Swap meets are also a fun and easy way to meet others in the hiking community.

Clothing

Clothes protect you against the elements and also help to regulate body temperature. What you wear when you go hiking should keep you dry and comfortable, no matter what the weather and season. From underwear to outerwear, pick garments that offer good "breathability." Wool blends and the new breed of synthetic microfibers do a good job at wicking moisture away from the skin. Shirts and pants made from microfiber polyesters are also extra-light and stretchy, allowing for maximum range of movement.

You will also want to dress in layers: underwear, one or more intermediate layers, and, finally, an outer layer. Wearing multiple layers of clothing offers you lots of flexibility for regulating body temperature and exposure. Test your clothing at different temperatures and levels of activity to find out what works best for you.

Rain Gear

Coastal currents smashing up against weather fronts dropping south from Canada give New England its famously fickle weather. Especially in summer, a sunny late morning start to your hike could mean a return trip in a raging rainstorm, often with very little warning time. No matter where you go or how long you expect to be out on the trail, bring along rain gear. It doesn't need to be elaborate: a vinyl foul weather poncho left in its packaging until needed is a compact addition to your pack.

If you do end up getting caught in a thunderstorm or sudden downpour, move away from high ground and tall trees immediately. Take shelter in a low spot, ravine, or thin place in the woods, cover up with your poncho, and wait for the storm to pass. Also,

HIKING GEAR CHECKLIST

Long-distance backpackers need to worry about hauling along camping and cooking equipment, but besides good boots, comfortable clothes, water, food, and a trusty map, it doesn't take much to have all the gear you need for a day hike. Here are some must-haves for your next outing.

IN CASE OF EMERGENCY

Altimeter

Compass

Extra clothes

First-aid kit

Lightweight (or mylar) blanket

Pen/pencil and paper

Swiss army-style knife

Waterproof matches

CREATURE COMFORTS

Binoculars

Bird, wildlife, and tree/flower identification guides

Bug spray/sunscreen

Camera

Face cloths

Fishing pole and fishing license

Picnic supplies

Trekking pole

And, of course, bring along your hiking guide!

---

look carefully at your surroundings, making sure you are not standing in a dry riverbed or wash while waiting, in case of flash floods.

Being out in rainy weather is also a concern for your feet and legs. Brushing up against wet ferns or low-lying plants can make for uncomfortably damp pant legs and soaked socks and boots. In case you do get stuck in the rain, another good piece of equipment to have on hand is a pair of gaiters, leggings made of Gore-Tex or other water-repellant materials. Gaiters are held in place under each boot with a stirrup and extend over your pants to just below the knee.

Shoes and Socks

The most important piece of gear may be well-fitting, comfortable, supportive shoes or boots. Finding the right footwear requires trying on various models and walking around in them in the store before deciding. Everyone's feet are different, and shoes or boots that feel great on your friend won't necessarily fit you well. Deciding how heavy your footwear should be depends on variables like how often you hike, whether you easily injure feet or ankles, and how much weight you'll carry. My general recommendation is to hike in the most lightweight footwear that you find comfortable and adequately supportive.

There are three basic types of hiking boots. Sneaker-like trail shoes are adequate when you are hiking in a dry climate and on well-established paths. Traditional hiking boots, sometimes called trail hikers or trail boots, are constructed with a higher cut and slightly stiffer sole to provide support on steep inclines and muddy paths. Mountaineering boots are for those who might need to attach crampons for a better grip on glaciers or hard-packed snow on mountain hikes and rock or ice climbing. Mountaineering boots are built with a very stiff sole to give your feet and ankles support and protection as you climb more challenging terrain.

The hiking boot experts at L.L.Bean, New England's premier shopping destination for outdoor gear and equipment, recommend hikers consider the various advantages of fabric-and-leather boots and all-leather boots. Fabric-and-leather boots are lighter and easier to break in, but all-leather boots offer added protection and durability in rigorous terrain, as well as being water resistant and breathable. Quality boots can be found in either style.

HIKING BOOTS

Try boots on at the end of the day when your feet are more swollen and wear the socks you plan to wear on the trail. Boots should feel snug but comfortable, so you can still wiggle your toes. Most hiking boots won't feel as instantly comfortable as sneakers, but they shouldn't pinch, cause hot spots, or constrict circulation. They should fit securely around your ankle and instep. Try walking down an incline at the store. Your feet should not slide forward, nor should your toenails scrape against the front of your boot. If your foot slides forward, the boot could be too wide. If the back of your heel moves around, your boots might not be laced up tight enough.

Once you purchase a pair of boots, break them in slowly with short hikes. Leather boots in particular take a while to break in, so take a couple of two- or three-hour hikes before your big trip or wear them around the house. If you find any sharp pressure points, use leather conditioner to soften the leather.

SOCKS

With exertion, one foot can sweat up to two pints of vapor/fluid per day. That's why wicking technology in hiking socks is so important. Without it, bacteria and fungus can become a problem. The best hiking socks are made from 100 percent wool or a wool blend of at least 50 percent wool. Unlike most synthetic fibers, which have to wait for moisture to condense into a liquid before wicking it away from your skin, wool socks absorb and transfer moisture in its vapor state, before it condenses. When it's hot, this creates a mini air-conditioning unit next to your feet, releasing heat through your socks and boots. And when it's cold, wicking keeps bone-chilling moisture at bay.

Some newer synthetics and synthetic blends are engineered to wick moisture; read the package label carefully and ask the store clerk for recommendations. The one fiber to stay away from is cotton, which absorbs water and perspiration and holds it next to your skin. If you are hiking with wet feet and the temperature drops below freezing, you risk getting frostbite. A good sock system and hiking boots reduce that possibility.

For comfort and good circulation, look for socks that won't bind your feet and avoid those made with excessive stitching or a scratchy knit that could lead to chafing. Terry woven socks are a good pick to distribute pressure and support your natural posture. And thicker isn't always better. Depending on the fit of your boots and the climate you'll be hiking in, a medium-weight wool sock that fits to mid-calf is often your best bet.

FOOTCARE

At an Appalachian Mountain Club hiking seminar, one instructor wisely noted that, besides the brain, "Your feet are the most important part of your body." Hurt any other

THE APPALACHIAN TRAIL

Perhaps the most famous hiking trail in the world, the Appalachian Trail (AT) runs 2,174 miles from Springer Mountain in Georgia to Mount Katahdin in Maine, along the spine of the Appalachian Mountains in 14 states. About 734 miles – or more than one-third – of the AT's length passes through five New England states: Connecticut (52 miles), Massachusetts (90 miles), Vermont (150 miles), New Hampshire (161 miles), and Maine (281 miles). New England boasts some of the AT's most spectacular, best-known, and rugged stretches, including the White Mountains, the southern Green Mountains, the Riga Plateau of Massachusetts and Connecticut, and Maine's Mahoosuc, Saddleback, and Bigelow ranges, 100-mile Wilderness, and Katahdin. A few hundred people hike the entire trail end to end every year, but thousands more take shorter backpacking trips and day hikes somewhere along the AT.

Maintained by hiking clubs that assume responsibility for different sections of the AT, the trail is well marked with signs and white blazes on trees and rocks above tree line. Shelters and campsites are spaced out along the AT so that backpackers have choices of where to spend each night. But those shelters can fill up during the busy season of summer and early fall, especially on weekends. The prime hiking season for the AT in New England depends on elevation and latitude, but generally, that season runs May–October in southern New England and mid-June–early October at higher elevations in northern New England.

body part and we might conceivably still make it home under our own power. Hurt our feet, and we're in trouble.

Take care of your feet. Wear clean socks that wick moisture from your skin while staying dry. Make sure your shoes or boots fit properly, are laced properly, and are broken in if they require it. Wear the appropriate footwear for the type of hiking you plan to do. If you anticipate your socks getting wet from perspiration or water, bring extra socks; on a multiday trip, have dry socks for each day, or at least change socks every other day. On hot days, roll your socks down over your boot tops to create what shoe manufacturers call "the chimney effect," cooling your feet by forcing air into your boots as you walk.

On longer treks, whenever you stop for a short rest on the trail—even if only for 5 or 10 minutes—sit down, pull off your boots and socks, and let them and your feet dry out. When backpacking, wash your feet at the end of the day. If you feel any hot spots developing, intervene before they progress into blisters. A slightly red or tender hot spot can be protected from developing into a blister with an adhesive bandage, tape, or a square of moleskin.

If a blister has formed, clean the area around it thoroughly to avoid infection. Sterilize a needle or knife in a flame, then pop and drain the blister to promote faster healing. Put an antiseptic ointment on the blister. Cut a piece of moleskin or Second Skin (both of which have a soft side and a sticky side with a peel-off backing) large enough to overlap the blistered area. Cut a hole as large as the blister out of the center of the moleskin, then place the moleskin over the blister so that the blister is visible through the hole. If done properly, you should be able to walk without aggravating the blister.

Backpack

When just out for the day, a roomy backpack will do to hold your belongings; toting an over-sized metal frame pack is not necessary unless you plan on camping overnight and need to bring along camp stove, bed roll, tent, and other extra gear. Shoulder straps should be foam padded for comfort. Look for backpacks made of water-resistant nylon. And just like clothes or shoes, try the pack on to make sure it has the fit you want.

Trekking Poles

For hikers who need a little extra physical support, trekking poles or walking sticks relieve feet and legs of tens of thousands of pounds of pressure over the course of an all-day hike. They are particularly useful in helping prevent knee and back pain from rigorous hiking. If you find a good walking stick along your journey, before heading back to your car, leave the stick in an obvious spot for another weary hiker to stumble upon. It warmed the bottom of my heart one day to find at least a dozen walking sticks leaning against a trailhead signpost in Massachusetts, free for anyone to use.

CLIMATE

With New England's biggest peaks in the northern states and its smaller hills and flatlands in the southern states, as well as an ocean moderating the Seacoast climate, this region's fair-weather hikers can find a trail to explore virtually year-round. But the wildly varied character of hiking opportunities here also demands some basic knowledge of and preparation for hitting the trails.

The ocean generally keeps coastal areas a little warmer in winter and cooler in summer than inland areas. Otherwise, any time of year, average temperatures typically grow cooler as you gain elevation or move northward.

New England's prime hiking season stretches for several months from spring through fall, with the season's length depending on the region. In general, summer high temperatures range 60°F–90°F with lows from 50°F to around freezing at higher elevations. Days are often humid in the forests and lower elevations and windy on the mountaintops. July and August see occasional thunderstorms, but July through September is the driest period. August is usually the best month for finding ripe wild blueberries along many trails, especially in northern New England.

September is often the best month for hiking, with dry, comfortable days, cool nights, and few bugs. Fall foliage colors peak anywhere from mid-September or early October in northern New England to early or mid-October in the south; by choosing your destinations well and moving north to south, you can hike through vibrant foliage for three or four successive weekends. The period from mid-October into November offers cool days, cold nights, no bugs, few people, and often little snow.

In the higher peaks of Vermont's Green Mountains, New Hampshire's White Mountains, Maine's northern Appalachians, and along the Appalachian Trail in parts of western Massachusetts and Connecticut, high-elevation snow disappears and alpine wildflowers bloom in late spring; by late October, wintry winds start blowing and snow starts flying (though it can snow above 4,000 feet in any month of the year). Spring trails are muddy at low elevations—some are closed to hiking during the April/May "mud season"—and buried under deep, slushy snow up high, requiring snowshoes. Winter conditions set in by mid-November and can become very severe, even life threatening.

CROSS-COUNTRY SKIING AND SNOWSHOEING

Many hikes in this book are great for cross-country skiing or snowshoeing in winter. But added precaution is needed. Days are short and the temperature may start to plummet by mid-afternoon, so carry the right clothing and don't overestimate how far you can travel in winter. Depending on snow conditions and your own fitness level and experience with either snowshoes or skis, a winter outing can take much longer than anticipated – and certainly much longer than a trip of similar distance on groomed trails at a cross-country ski resort. Breaking your own trail through fresh snow can also be very exhausting – take turns leading and conserve energy by following the leader's tracks, which also serve as a good return trail.

The proper clothing becomes essential in winter, especially the farther you wander from roads. Wear a base layer that wicks moisture from your skin and dries quickly, middle layers that insulate and do not retain moisture, and a windproof shell that breathes well and is waterproof or water-resistant (the latter type of garment usually breathes much better than something that's completely waterproof). Size boots to fit over a thin, synthetic liner sock and a thicker, heavyweight synthetic-blend sock. For your hands, often the most versatile system consists of gloves and/or mittens that also can be layered, with an outer layer that's waterproof and windproof and preferably also breathable.

Most importantly, don't overdress: Remove layers if you're getting too hot. Avoid becoming wet with perspiration, which can lead to too much cooling. Drink plenty of fluids and eat snacks frequently to maintain your energy level; feeling tired or cold on a winter outing may be an indication of dehydration or hunger.

As long as you're safe, cautious, and aware, winter is a great time to explore New England's trails. Have fun out there.

Going above the tree line in winter is considered a mountaineering experience by many (though these mountains lack glacier travel and high altitude), so be prepared for harsh cold and strong winds.

The second strongest wind gust ever recorded on Earth was measured on April 12, 1934, at the weather observatory on the summit of New Hampshire's Mount Washington. The gust was clocked at 231 mph. The summit of Mount Washington remains in clouds 60 percent of the time. Its average temperature year-round is 26.5°F; winds average 35 mph and exceed hurricane force (75 mph) on average 104 days a year. Be aware that in the higher peaks of the Whites as well as alpine peaks in Vermont and Maine, weather conditions change rapidly. It is not uncommon to set off from the trailhead in hot, sunny weather only to hit driving rain and hail on the summit.

In the smaller hills and flatlands of central and southern New England, the snow-free hiking season often begins by early spring and lasts into late autumn. Some of these trails are even occasionally free of snow during the winter, or offer opportunities for snowshoeing or cross-country skiing in woods protected from strong winds, with warmer temperatures than you'll find on the bigger peaks up north. Many Seacoast trails, even in Maine, rarely stay snow-covered all winter, though they can get occasional heavy snowfall and be very icy in cold weather. For more information about weather-related trail conditions, refer to the individual hike listings.

SAFETY AND FIRST AID

Few of us would consider hiking a high-risk activity. But like any physical activity, it does pose certain risks, and it's up to us to minimize them. For starters, make sure your physical condition is adequate for your objective—the quickest route to injury is over-extending either your skills or your physical abilities. You wouldn't presume that you could rock climb a 1,000-foot cliff if you've never climbed before; don't assume you're ready for one of New England's hardest hikes if you've never—or not very recently—done anything nearly as difficult.

Build up your fitness level by gradually increasing your workouts and the length of your hikes. Beyond strengthening muscles, you must strengthen the soft connective tissue in joints like knees and ankles that are too easily strained and take weeks or months to heal from injury. Staying active in a variety of activities—hiking, running, bicycling, Nordic skiing—helps develop good overall fitness and decreases the likelihood of an overuse injury. Most importantly, stretch muscles before and after a workout to reduce the chance of injury.

New England's most rugged trails—and even parts of its more moderate paths—can be very rocky and steep. Uneven terrain is often a major contributor to falls resulting in serious, acute injury. Most of us have a fairly reliable self-preservation instinct—and you should trust it. If something strikes you as dangerous or beyond your abilities, don't try it, or simply wait until you think you're ready for it.

An injury far from a road also means it may be hours before the victim reaches a hospital. Basic training in wilderness first aid is beneficial to anyone who frequents the mountains, even recreational hikers. New England happens to have two highly respected sources for such training, and the basic course requires just one weekend. Contact SOLO (Conway, NH, 603/447-6711, www.soloschools.com) or Wilderness Medical Associates (Scarborough, ME, 207/730-7331, www.wildmed.com) for information.

Plants

From fern-choked forest floors to fields filled with wild blueberries, plant life in New England is varied and diverse. And luckily, there are only a few poisonous plant species to be wary of: poison ivy, poison oak, and poison sumac. The three plants contain urushiol, an oil that causes an allergic reaction and rash in humans. According to the American Academy of Dermatology, humans typically come in contact with urushiol by brushing up against or touching the plants, touching an object or animal that has come in contact with the oil, or breathing in urushiol particles if a poison plant is burned in a campfire.

Urushiol penetrates the skin in minutes, but the rash usually takes anywhere from 12 to 72 hours to appear, followed quickly by severe itching, redness, swelling, and even blisters. When the rash develops, streaks or lines often reveal where the plant brushed against the skin. A rash triggered by urushiol does not spread and is not contagious.

Recognizing Poisonous Plants

Hikers best protection against the itchy rash caused by urushiol is learning how to identify the plants that contain the oil.

Poison Ivy: Leaves of three, let them be... Poison ivy grows as vines or low shrubs almost everywhere in New England and true to that famous phrase from summer camp, the plant consists of three pointed leaflets; the middle leaflet has a much longer stalk than the two side ones. Leaflets are reddish when they bud in spring, turn green during the summer, and then become various shades of yellow, orange, or red in the autumn. Small greenish flowers grow in bunches attached to the main stem close to where each leaf joins it. Later in the season, clusters of poisonous berries form. They are whitish, with a waxy look.

Poison Oak: There are two main species of poison oak, but the species commonly found in New England is the Atlantic Poison Oak a vine plant or bush. Poison oak leaves grow in clusters of three leaves; the lobbed appearance of each leaf resembles the white oak. Plants put out berries in spring that are white or yellowish-green in color and leaflets change color with the seasons. Poison oak tends to grow in sandy soils.

Poison Sumac: Though it is one of New England's native tree species, poison sumac is the rarest of the urushiol-containing plants. Sumac can be identified by its row of paired leaflets that contains an additional leaflet at the end. Often the leaves have spots that resemble blotches of black enamel paint. These spots are actually urushiol, which when exposed to air turn brownish-black. Poison sumac tends to grow near wet areas and bogs.

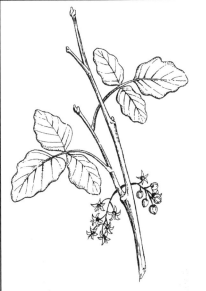

Avoiding Poison Oak: Remember the old Boy Scout saying: "Leaves of three, let them be."

TREATING POISON IVY, POISON OAK, AND POISON SUMAC

When an allergic reaction develops, the skin should be washed well with lukewarm water and soap. All clothing should be laundered, and everything else that may be contaminated with urushiol should be washed thoroughly. Urushiol can remain active for a long time. For mild cases, cool showers and an over-the-counter product that eases itching can be effective. Oatmeal baths and baking-soda mixtures also can soothe the discomfort. When a severe reaction develops contact a dermatologist immediately, or go to an emergency room. Prescription medication may be needed to reduce the swelling and itch.

Insects

Black flies, or mayflies, emerge by late April or early May and pester hikers until late June or early July, while mosquitoes come out in late spring and dissipate (but do not disappear) by midsummer. No-see-ums (tiny biting flies that live up to their name) plague some wooded areas in summer. Of particular concern in recent years has been the small, but growing number of cases of eastern equine encephalitis (EEE) in humans, spread by EEE-infected mosquitoes. It's still very rare, but cases of EEE tend to emerge each year at the end of summer and early fall. Mosquitoes acquire EEE through contact with diseased birds.

LYME DISEASE

Deer ticks are often carriers of the bacteria that causes Lyme disease. Hundreds of cases of the disease – most mild and treatable with antibiotics – are diagnosed in New England each year. The easiest way to avoid tick bites is to wear socks, long pants, and a long-sleeve shirt whenever you hike, and especially when you hike in areas with tall grass and/or large deer populations. Tucking your pant legs into your socks prevents the best protection against the tiny ticks, but never fail to check your skin thoroughly at the end of a hike. Most tick bites cause a sharp sting, but some may go unnoticed.

If you do find a tick, don't panic. Take a pair of tweezers and place them around the tick as close to your skin as possible. Gently pull the tick straight out to avoid parts of it breaking off still attached to the skin. The majority of tick bites are no more of a nuisance than a mosquito or black fly bite. If you do notice a rash spreading out from around the bite within a week of finding the tick, it may be an early sign of Lyme disease. Other symptoms are similar to the flu – headache, fever, muscle soreness, neck stiffness, or nausea – and may appear anywhere from a few days to a week or so after being bitten. If you do notice any symptoms, seek medical help immediately. When caught in its early stages, Lyme disease is easily treated with antibiotics; left untreated, the disease can be debilitating.

You will want to have some kind of bug repellant with you no matter where your hike takes you. (Even the windswept coast isn't free of insects; New England's swarms of black flies first appear on the coast and then move inland.) There is much debate about the health effects of wearing sprays containing the chemical DEET; some may prefer ointments made with essential oils and herbs believed to deter bugs. Or skip the sprays and salves and wear a lightweight jacket made of head-to-waist (or head-to-toe) mosquito netting. These unusual creations are made by Bug Baffler, a New Hampshire-based company, and sold on the web (www.bugbaffler.com).

Wildlife

The remarkable recovery of New England's mountains and forests during the past century from the abuses of the logging industry has spawned a boom in the populations of many wild animals, from increased numbers of black bears and moose to the triumphant return of the bald eagle and peregrine falcon. For the most part, you don't have to worry about your safety in the backcountry when it comes to wildlife encounters. It's typical for hikers to see lots of scat and a traffic jam of prints on the trail without ever actually spotting the animals that left this evidence behind.

Still, a few sensible precautions are in order. If you're camping in the backcountry, know how to hang or store your food properly to keep it from bears and smaller animals like mice, which are more likely to be a problem. You certainly should never approach the region's two largest mammals: moose, which you may see in northern New England, or bear, which you may never see. These creatures are wild and unpredictable, and a moose can weigh several hundred pounds and put the hurt on a much smaller human. The greatest danger posed by moose is that of hitting one while driving on dark back roads at night; hundreds of collisions occur in Maine and New Hampshire every year, often wrecking vehicles and injuring people. At night, drive more slowly than you would during daylight. As one forest ranger warns, "the most dangerous part of hiking in the mountains is the drive to the trailhead."

First Aid
HYPOTHERMIA
In humans and other warm-blooded animals, core body temperature is maintained near a constant level through internal temperature regulation. When the body is over-exposed to cold, however, internal mechanisms may be unable to replenish excessive heat loss. Hypothermia is defined as any body temperature below 95°F (35 °C). Despite its association with winter, hypothermia can occur even when the air temperature is in the 50s. Often the victim has gotten wet or over-exerted himself or herself on the trail. Hypothermia is a leading cause of death in the outdoors.

Symptoms of hypothermia include uncontrollable shivering, weakness, loss of coordination, confusion, cold skin, drowsiness, frost bite, and slowed breathing or heart rate. If a member of your hiking party demonstrates one or more of these symptoms, send a call out for help and take action immediately. Get out of the wind and cold and seek shelter in a warm, dry environment. Help the victim change into windproof, waterproof clothes and wrap up in a blanket, if one is available; start a fire to add extra warmth. Encourage the victim to eat candy, energy bars, and other high-sugar foods to boost energy. Do not offer alcohol, it only makes heat loss worse.

Victims of mild to moderate hypothermia may be suffering from impaired judgment and not be making rational decisions. They might try to resist help; be persistent.

HEAT STROKE
Our bodies produce a tremendous amount of internal heat. Under normal conditions, we cool ourselves by sweating and radiating heat through the skin. However, in certain circumstances, such as extreme heat, high humidity, or vigorous activity in the hot sun, this cooling system may begin to fail, allowing heat to build up to dangerous levels.

If a person becomes dehydrated and cannot sweat enough to cool their body, their internal temperature may rise to dangerously high levels, causing heat stroke. Symptoms include headache, mental confusion, and cramps throughout the entire body. If you have these symptoms, or notice them in a member of your hiking party, take immediate action to lower the body's core temperature. Get out of the sun and move to a shadier location. Pour water over the victim and fan the skin to stimulate sweating; sit in a nearby stream, if possible. Encourage the victim to drink liquids and rest. If symptoms are severe or don't improve within a few minutes of starting first aid, do not hesitate to call for help.

Probably the most effective way to cut risk for heat stroke is to stay adequately hydrated. When the temperatures soar on a New England summer day, stop frequently on the trail for water and rest breaks.

SPRAINS AND BREAKS
For any sprain or strain, remember RICE: rest, ice, compression, elevation. First, have the patient rest by lying down on the ground or nearest flat surface. Next, reduce swelling by gently placing a plastic freezer bag filled with cold water on the injury. To compress the ankle, snugly wrap the injury in an ACE bandage. (First-aid tape will also work.)

The wrap should cover the entire foot except for the heel and end several inches above the ankle. Most compression wraps are self-fastening or come with clip fasteners—or use tape to secure the end. If toes become purplish or blue, cool to the touch, or feel numb or tingly according to the patient, the wrap is too tight and should be loosened.

Keep the leg elevated until swelling is visibly reduced. When you or someone you are with suffers a sprained ankle or other minor injury on the trail, keep an open mind about finishing the hike. Because it's always more enjoyable when everyone can fully participate, it might be best to cut your losses and come back another time.

Navigational Tools

At some point, almost every hiker becomes lost. Torn down trail signs, trail detours, faded blazes, and snow, fog, and other conditions can make staying the course very rough going. First, take every step to prevent becoming lost. Before you hike, study a map of the area to become familiar with the trails, nearby roads, streams, mountains and other features. Leave a trip plan with family or friends and sign in at the trailhead register or nearby ranger cabin, if a hiker registry is available.

Always hike with a map and compass. And as you ramble along the trail, observe the topography around you (ridges, recognizable summits, rivers, etc.). They serve as good reference points, particularly when you are above the tree line. Some hikers leave small piles of rocks spaced at regular intervals to help them navigate treeless, alpine areas. Should you become disoriented, stop, pull out your map and look at the countryside for familiar landmarks.

Few people remain truly lost after consulting a map and calmly studying the terrain for five minutes. If you still need help orienting yourself, you may want to head to a ridge or high ground so you can identify hills or streams that are marked on your topographical map. Lay your map on the ground and put your compass on top to orient north. Another helpful gadget is an altimeter, which can tell you your approximate elevation; you can then pinpoint this elevation on a topographic map. Until you have your bearings, don't wander too far from your original route. If you told family members or fellow hikers where you plan to hike, that area is where rescuers will start searching for you.

Should you continue to be lost, S.T.O.P. (stop, think, observe, and plan). And don't panic. Not only does it cloud your judgment, you will be using up energy that you may need later on. Stay put and, if you carry a whistle, blow it at timed intervals to signal rescuers or other hikers (yelling also works).

HIKING ETHICS
Trail Etiquette

One of the great things about hiking is the quality of the people you meet on the trail. Hikers generally do not need an explanation of the value of courtesy, and one hopes this will always ring true. Still, with the popularity of hiking on the increase, and thousands of new hikers taking to the trails of New England every year, it's a good idea to brush up on some etiquette basics.

As a general rule and a friendly favor to other hikers, yield the trail to others whether you're going uphill or down. All trail users should yield to horses by stepping aside for the safety of everyone present. Likewise, horseback riders should, whenever possible, avoid situations where their animals are forced to push past hikers on very narrow trails.

Mountain bikers should yield to hikers, announce their approach, and pass nonbikers slowly. During hunting season, nonhunters should wear blaze orange, or an equally bright, conspicuous color. The hunters you may come across on the trail are usually responsible and friendly and deserve like treatment.

Many of us enjoy the woods and mountains for the quiet, and we should keep that in mind on the trail, at summits, or backcountry campsites. Many of us share the belief that things like cell phones, radios, and CD players do not belong in the mountains. High tech devices may also pose serious safety risks when used on the trail. Texting while hiking? Not a good idea when you should be watching out for exposed tree roots and rocky footing. Likewise, listening to a MP3 player could prevent you from hearing another hiker alerting you to dangers ahead.

New England has seen some conflict between hikers and mountain bikers, but it's important to remember that solutions to those issues are never reached through hostility and rudeness. Much more is accomplished when we begin from a foundation of mutual respect and courtesy. After all, we're all interested in preserving and enjoying our trails.

Large groups have a disproportionate impact on backcountry campsites and on the experience of other people. Be aware of and respect any restrictions on group size. Even where no regulation exists, keep your group size to no more than 10 people.

TIPS FOR AVOIDING CROWDS

Even on New England's most popular peaks, it is still possible to beat the crowds and have the trail all—or mostly—to yourself. Timing is everything. For hikes of less than six or seven miles round-trip, try to arrive at the trailhead early in the morning. Depending on the elevation gain, a seven-mile round-tripper will take the average hiker somewhere around three hours to complete—the perfect length for a late morning or early afternoon trek. Start your hike by 7 A.M. on a sunny Saturday morning and you will probably be returning to your car just as the weekend crush is arriving. For very short hikes, waiting until late afternoon or early evening before hitting the trail almost always ensures low boot traffic. But keep these late day hikes short and to destinations with easy footing just in case you're still out on the trail when night falls.

For very long hikes of nine miles round-trip or more, this early-bird strategy will not work, since early morning is the normal start time for most longer hikes. To still salvage a little solitude on your journey, you might want to consider breaking high mileage hikes into a two-day trek with an overnight stay at a shelter or backcountry campground. Start out on the trail later in the day and aim to camp at least halfway to the summit (within a mile of the summit is ideal). As early as you can the next day, finish the climb and enjoy the peaceful stillness.

Another way to avoid the crowds is to hike during the work week, when even the busiest of New England's trailheads are almost empty. If it felt as though you were part of a conga line climbing to the top of Mount Washington on a warm, sunny Sunday afternoon, come back on Wednesday and find almost no one around. Similarly, time your hikes according to the seasons. With the exception of a few places in northern New England that tend to stay muddy and even icy well into late spring, June is often the best month for encountering light boot traffic. Birds chirp, the air is fresh, wildflowers bloom in the meadows, and the throngs of summer tourists—and swarms of mosquitoes—have yet to arrive. Similarly, the week after Labor Day weekend is often quiet on the trail, with family vacationers gone back to school and the fall foliage season not yet underway.

Hiking with Children

Exploring the great outdoors with kids is one of life's great rewards. Starting from a very young age, a baby can be placed in a front carrier and taken out on almost any trail where the walking is flat and the environment serene; the rhythmic pace of hiking tends to lull even the fussiest of infants right to sleep. Backpack carriers are a good way to tote toddlers on-trail and, depending on the model, can accommodate a child of up to 35 pounds. When hiking with a child-carrier pack, keep a small mirror in your pocket so you can frequently check on your passenger without having to stop and remove the pack.

Around age three, kids are ready to hit the trail along with the rest of the family. But, little legs don't travel very far. Make your family outings kid-centric by picking short hikes that lead to such exciting features as waterfalls, duck-filled ponds, giant glacial erratics, huge gnarled tree trunks, beaver dams, and small hills with big views. Even if the hike is under a half mile in total length, plan extra time for rest stops and lots of unfettered exploration. Most children love the grown-up feel of having their own lightweight backpack; fill the pack with a water bottle and snack treats.

When a child reaches school age, physical ability rises dramatically. And so does his or her responsibility as a hiker. Teach your children how to read maps, how to use a compass, and what to do if lost. Show by example how to be courteous to the other hikers you encounter on the trail. Your efforts will be appreciated.

Hiking with Pets

Dogs are great trail companions and generally love the adventure of hiking every bit as much as their owners do. But dogs can create unnecessary friction in the backcountry. Dog owners should respect any regulations and not presume that strangers are eager to meet their pet. Keep your pet under physical control whenever other people are approaching. And for your dog's protection, always bring a leash along, even if regulations don't call for one.

Due to its large wildlife population, Baxter State Park in Maine is one notable destination that does not permit pets of any kind inside its borders. If you do have your dog along, check in with the campsites lining the access roads to Baxter. Many offer day boarding for dogs. Several bird refuges and Audubon sanctuaries also prohibit dogs. Call ahead to these and other destinations to find out trail regulations for pets.

Leave No Trace

Many of New England's trails receive heavy use, making it imperative that we all understand how to minimize our physical impact on the land. The nonprofit organization Leave No Trace (LNT) advocates a set of principles for low-impact backcountry use that are summarized in these basic guidelines:
- Be considerate of other visitors.
- Dispose of waste properly.
- Leave what you find.
- Minimize campfire impact.
- Plan ahead and prepare.

• Respect wildlife.
• Travel and camp on durable surfaces.
LNT offers more in-depth guidelines for low-impact camping and hiking on its website: www.lnt.org. You can also contact them by mail or phone: Leave No Trace Inc., P.O. Box 997, Boulder, CO 80306; 303/442-8222 or 800/332-4100.

Camping

The following are more recommendations that apply to many backcountry areas in New England:

• Avoid building campfires; cook with a backpacking stove. If you do build a campfire, use only wood found locally as a way to prevent the spread of destructive forest pests introduced from areas outside New England. In all six states, campers are encouraged not to move firewood more than 50 miles from its original source. Store-bought, packaged firewood is usually okay, as long as it is labeled "kiln dried" or "USDA Certified." Wood that is kiln dried is generally free of pests, although if the wood is not heated to a certain temperature, insects can survive.
• Avoid trails that are very muddy in spring; that's when they are most susceptible to erosion.
• Bury human waste beneath six inches of soil at least 200 feet from any water source.
• Burn and bury, or carry out, used toilet paper.
• Carry out everything you carry in.
• Choose a campsite at least 200 feet from trails and water sources, unless you're using a designated site. Make sure your site bears no evidence of your stay when you leave.
• Do not leave any food behind, even buried, as animals will dig it up. Learn how to hang food appropriately to keep it from bears. Black bears have spread their range over much of New England in recent years, and problems have arisen in isolated backcountry areas where human use is heavy.
• Even biodegradable soap is harmful to the environment, so simply wash your cooking gear with water away from any streams or ponds.
• Last but not least, know and follow any regulations for the area you will be visiting.

THE BERKSHIRES

© JAROSLAW TRAPSZO

BEST HIKES

Less than a three-hour drive from both Boston and New York City, the rural hills and pastoral landscape of western Massachusetts offer little evidence that such large urban centers are so close by. This is a place where summit views miraculously still yield rolling farmland, quaint village skylines, and unbroken acres of forest; and where traffic jams often come in the form of wild turkeys slowly strutting across a backwoods trail.

The Berkshires region harbors the Bay State's highest peak, 3,491-foot Mount Greylock (technically a part of the Taconic Range), as well as other rugged mountains, including Monument Mountain and Mount Everett. The Appalachian Trail runs for 89 miles through the Berkshires, with such highlights as Mount Greylock and the beautiful Riga Plateau; both are popular destinations for day hiking and backpacking, especially July-September, when camping areas tend to fill up quickly on weekends. But both are also far enough south and low enough that the prime hiking season often begins by mid-spring and lasts through late autumn.

Fall color in the mixed hardwood forests of the Berkshires is spectacular. Foliage usually peaks around Columbus Day weekend, the perfect opportunity for a long weekend in the mountains. (Leaf peepers often use Stockbridge or Lenox as a homebase for outings — each is close to many of the area's most scenic trailheads.) Winters are typically cold and see plenty of snow in the hills. Several of the hikes included in this chapter make excellent, easy-to-moderate outings on snowshoes or cross-country skis.

Though the Appalachian Trail does tend to draw the heaviest hiker traffic, there's plenty of other fine hiking in western Massachusetts, from state forests with hidden gems like Alander Mountain and the Hubbard River Gorge to one of New England's most beautiful waterfalls, Bash Bish Falls. Lining the Connecticut River Valley is the much-loved Mount Tom and the multi-use Norwottuck rail trail, a bike path located near many of the area's colleges. Many of the trails in this rural region simply ramble through the woods and make for great wildlife viewing: hawks, owls, frogs, fish, beaver, otter, fox, gray squirrel, muskrats, white-tailed deer, snowshoe hares, and even the reclusive black bear all call this region home.

Along the Appalachian Trail, dogs must be kept under control, and bikes, horses, hunting, and firearms are prohibited. In state parks and forests, dogs must be leashed; horses are allowed in most state forests and parks, as is hunting in season.

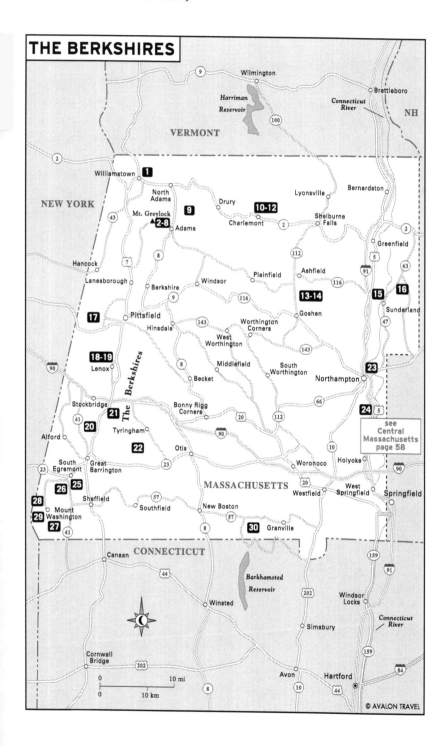

THE BERKSHIRES

1 PINE COBBLE
3.2 mi/2 hr

in Williamstown

Tucked away in the Bay State's northwest corner, the extensive quartzite ledges atop 1,894-foot Pine Cobble offer excellent views of the Hoosic Valley, including the low, green hills flanking the Hoosic River and towering Mount Greylock. Ascending at an easy to moderate grade, this 3.2-mile round-trip trek is popular with students at nearby Williams College and—like so many of the hikes in the Berkshire region—is an adventurous outing for young children. Passing through an unusual forest mix of oak and white pine, this hike nets an elevation gain of about 900 feet.

From the parking area, walk across Pine Cobble Road to the Pine Cobble Trail. Follow the trail's blue blazes and well-worn path. In less than a mile, pass a side path on the right leading 350 feet downhill to Bear Spring, a worthwhile detour. Continuing along the Pine Cobble Trail, at 1.5 miles from the parking area, the blue blazes hook sharply left and a spur path leads to the right 0.1 mile to Pine Cobble's summit. Take the spur path, soon reaching a ledge with views west to the Taconic Range. About 100 feet farther uphill is the summit. The best views are from the open ledges about 30 feet beyond the summit. Looking south (right) you see Mount Greylock; east lie the Clarksburg State Forest's woods and hills; and to the north extends an array of hills traversed by Appalachian Trail hikers on their way into Vermont. Return the same way you came.

Special note: Hikers interested in a longer outing can continue north on the Pine Cobble Trail 0.5 mile to the Appalachian Trail, turn left (north), and hike another 0.5 mile to a view south of Mount Greylock from Eph's Lookout. The added distance makes the entire round-trip 5.2 miles.

User Groups: Hikers and dogs. This trail is not suitable for bikes or horses; no wheelchair facilities.

Permits: Parking and access are free.

Maps: A map of area trails is available from the Appalachian Mountain Club (Northern Berkshires/Southwestern Massachusetts/Wachusett Mountain, $5.95). For a topographic area map, request North Adams from the USGS.

Directions: From the junction of U.S. 7 and Route 2 in Williamstown, drive east on Route 2 for 0.6 mile, then turn left on Cole Avenue at the first traffic light. Drive another 0.8 mile, crossing a bridge over the Hoosic River and railroad tracks and then turn right on North Housac Road. Follow it 0.4 mile to a left turn onto Pine Cobble Road and continue to the parking area 0.2 mile up on the left, across the street from the trailhead.

GPS Coordinates: 42.7157 N, 73.1849 W

Contact: Williamstown Rural Lands Foundation, 671 Cold Spring Rd., Williamstown, MA 01267, 413/458-2494, www.wrlf.org.

2 MOUNT GREYLOCK: MONEY BROOK FALLS
5 mi/3 hr

in Mount Greylock State Reservation in Williamstown, North Adams, Adams, and Lanesborough

Money Brook Falls tumbles from an impressive height of 40 feet into a ravine choked with trees that haven't survived the steep, erosive terrain. Despite being one of the most spectacular natural features on the biggest hill in the Bay State, it is also among Massachusetts's best-kept secrets. Keeping foot traffic light could be the trail's several stream crossings, some of which can be difficult in high water, especially in late spring when the falls are at their viewing peak.

From the parking area, walk past the gate onto the Hopper Trail and follow a flat, grassy lane for 0.2 mile. Where the Hopper Trail diverges right, continue straight ahead on the

© JAROSLAW TRAPSZO

Money Brook Falls on Mount Greylock

Money Brook Trail (look for the trail marker). The trail ascends gently at first, but after passing the Mount Prospect Trail junction at 1.5 miles, it goes through some short, steep stretches. At 2.4 miles, turn right onto a side path that leads 0.1 mile to the falls. Hike back the way you came.

There is a lean-to and a dispersed backcountry camping zone along the Money Brook Trail.

User Groups: Hikers and leashed dogs. No horses, bikes, or wheelchair facilities.

Permits: A daily fee of $2 is collected mid-May–mid-October at some parking areas.

Maps: Find free, basic trail maps of Mount Greylock State Reservation at the park visitors center or online at the Massachusetts Division of State Parks and Recreation website. A map of area trails is available from the Appalachian Mountain Club (Northern Berkshires/Southwestern Massachusetts/Wachusett Mountain, $5.95). For topographic area maps,

request North Adams and Cheshire from the USGS.

Directions: From Route 43 in Williamstown, 2.5 miles south of the junction of Routes 43 and 2 and 2.3 miles north of the junction of Route 43 and U.S. 7, turn east onto Hopper Road at a sign for Mount Hope Park. Drive 1.4 miles and bear left onto a dirt road. Continue 0.7 mile to the parking area on the right.

From the mid-December close of hunting season through mid-May, roads within the state reservation are closed to vehicles (and groomed for snowmobiles), but Hopper Road is maintained to this trailhead.

GPS Coordinates: 42.6546 N, 73.1986 W

Contact: Mount Greylock State Reservation, P.O. Box 138, Rockwell Rd., Lanesborough, MA 01237, 413/499-4262 or 413/499-4263. Massachusetts Division of State Parks and Recreation, 251 Causeway St., Suite 600, Boston, MA 02114-2104, 617/626-1250, www.mass.gov/dcr/parks/mtGreylock.

❸ MOUNT GREYLOCK CIRCUIT

12 mi/8 hr   🏃5 ⛰10

in Mount Greylock State Reservation in Williamstown, North Adams, Adams, and Lanesborough

A long, scenic loop around the highest peak in Massachusetts, 3,491-foot Mount Greylock, this 12-mile circuit takes in as many of the mountain's best features as possible on a day hike. Climb through and around the spectacular glacial cirque known as the Hopper, pass two waterfalls, travel over the summit, follow a stretch of the Appalachian Trail, and then descend through the rugged ravine of beautiful Money Brook. You can shave the distance by two miles by skipping the side trail to March Cataract Falls, and another mile by skipping Robinson Point. This entire hike gains more than 2,500 feet in elevation.

From the parking area, walk past the gate

onto the Hopper Trail and follow a flat, grassy lane 0.2 mile to a junction with the Money Brook Trail. Bear right with the Hopper Trail, ascending an old, and sometimes steep logging road, another two miles until you reach Sperry Road. Turn left and walk the road 0.1 mile; just before the parking area on the right, turn left on a dirt campground road. Walk about 200 feet, past the Chimney Group Camping Area, and turn left at a sign for the March Cataract Falls Trail. It leads a mile, descending through switchbacks, to March Cataract Falls, a 30-foot falls that usually maintains a flow even during dry seasons.

Backtrack to Sperry Road, turn left, walk about 100 yards past the parking area, and then turn left at a sign onto the Hopper Trail. The wide path climbs at a moderate grade past a short falls. Where the Deer Hill Trail diverges right, bear left to stay on the Hopper Trail. Within a mile of Sperry Road, where the Hopper Trail makes a sharp right, turn left onto the Overlook Trail. You reach the first view of the Hopper within minutes, though trees partially obstruct it. A half mile down the Overlook Trail lies the second view, which is better; Stony Ledge is visible across the Hopper to the west. Continue on the Overlook Trail to the paved Notch Road, 1.2 miles from the Hopper Trail junction. Turn left and walk the road downhill 0.1 mile, past a day-use parking turnout, then turn left onto a trail marked by blue blazes. It descends steeply 0.2 mile to Robinson Point and a view of the Hopper superior to anything on the Overlook Trail. Double back to the Overlook Trail, cross Notch Road, and follow the Overlook Trail uphill for 0.4 mile to the white-blazed Appalachian Trail (AT). Turn left on the AT, following it across the parking lot to the summit, where you find the War Memorial Tower and the Bascom Lodge. The best views are to the east from the meadow beyond the tower; there are also good views to the west.

From the tower, follow the AT north. About a mile from the summit is a good eastern view. About 2.4 miles from the summit, a side trail

© JAROSLAW TRAPSZO

War Memorial Tower at the summit of Mount Greylock

leads left to Notch Road, but continue 0.2 mile straight ahead on the AT over Mount Williams, one of Greylock's secondary summits. The AT swings left here, descending easily 0.9 mile to Notch Road. Cross the road and, after 0.1 mile in the woods, turn left onto the Money Brook Trail; in 0.2 mile, pass a short side path leading to the Wilbur's Clearing shelter. The trail reaches a side path 0.7 mile beyond the shelter that leads a short distance to rugged Money Brook Falls. Backtrack from the falls on the side path and continue on the Money Brook Trail, following the brook through a wild, narrow valley, with a few crossings that could be tricky in high water. Nearly a mile past the falls, the Mount Prospect Trail branches right; stay on the Money Brook Trail another 1.5 miles to the Hopper Trail; continue straight ahead on the Hopper Trail 0.2 mile back to the parking area.

There is a lean-to and a dispersed backcountry camping zone along the Money Brook Trail.

User Groups: Hikers and leashed dogs. This trail should not be attempted in winter except by hikers prepared for severe winter weather. No bikes, horses, or wheelchair facilities.

Permits: A daily fee of $2 is collected mid-May–mid-October at some parking areas.

Maps: Find free, basic trail maps of Mount Greylock State Reservation at the park visitors center or online at the Massachusetts Division of State Parks and Recreation website. A map of area trails is available from the Appalachian Mountain Club (Northern Berkshires/Southwestern Massachusetts/Wachusett Mountain, $5.95). For topographic area maps, request North Adams and Cheshire from the USGS.

Directions: From Route 43 in Williamstown, 2.5 miles south of the junction of Routes 43 and 2 in Williamstown and 2.3 miles north of the junction of Route 43 and U.S. 7, turn east onto Hopper Road at a sign for Mount Hope Park. Drive 1.4 miles and bear left onto a dirt road. Continue 0.7 mile to the parking area on the right.

From the mid-December close of hunting season through mid-May, roads within the state reservation are closed to vehicles (and groomed for snowmobiles), but Hopper Road is maintained to this trailhead.

GPS Coordinates: 42.6546 N, 73.1986 W

Contact: Mount Greylock State Reservation, P.O. Box 138, Rockwell Rd., Lanesborough, MA 01237, 413/499-4262 or 413/499-4263. Massachusetts Division of State Parks and Recreation, 251 Causeway St., Suite 600, Boston, MA 02114-2104, 617/626-1250, www.mass.gov/dcr/parks/mtGreylock.

4 MOUNT GREYLOCK: ROBINSON POINT

0.4 mi/0.5 hr ♟₂ △₉

in Mount Greylock State Reservation in Williamstown, North Adams, Adams, and Lanesborough

The high ledge at Robinson Point offers one of the best views of the Hopper, the huge glacial cirque carved into Mount Greylock's northwest flank. Visible from the ledge are Stony Ledge, at the end of the ridge forming the Hopper's western wall; Williamstown, in the valley beyond the Hopper's mouth; and the Taconic Range on the horizon. This very short trek is not too easy: the trail's steep descent could be a bit too hard on the knees for some hikers.

From the parking turnout on Notch Road, walk downhill just a few steps and then turn left onto a trail marked by blue blazes. It descends a very steep 0.2 mile to Robinson Point. Return the same way.

User Groups: Hikers and leashed dogs. This trail is not suitable for horses. Bikes are prohibited; no wheelchair facilities.

Permits: A daily fee of $2 is collected mid-May–mid-October at some parking areas.

Maps: Find free, basic trail maps of Mount Greylock State Reservation at the park visitors center or online at the Massachusetts Division of State Parks and Recreation website. A map of area trails is available from the Appalachian Mountain Club (Northern Berkshires/Southwestern Massachusetts/Wachusett Mountain, $5.95). For topographic area maps, request North Adams and Cheshire from the USGS.

Directions: From Route 2 in Williamstown, 3.7 miles east of the junction of Routes 2 and 43, turn south onto Notch Road. Follow Notch Road up the mountain for 7.4 miles to a turnout for day-use parking on the right. From U.S. 7 in Lanesborough, 1.3 miles north of town center and 4.2 miles south of the Lanesborough/New Ashford line, turn east onto North Main Street. Drive 0.7 mile and turn right onto Quarry Road. Continue 0.6 mile and bear left at a sign reading Rockwell Road to Greylock. The Greylock Visitor Center is 0.6 mile farther up that road. From the visitors center, follow Rockwell Road up the mountain for 7.2 miles, turn left onto Notch Road, and continue 0.9 mile to the day-use parking turnout on the left.

From the mid-December close of hunting

season through mid-May, roads within the state reservation are closed to vehicles (and groomed for snowmobiles). This trailhead is not accessible by car in the winter months. GPS Coordinates: 42.6416 N, 73.1660 W
Contact: Mount Greylock State Reservation, P.O. Box 138, Rockwell Rd., Lanesborough, MA 01237, 413/499-4262 or 413/499-4263. Massachusetts Division of State Parks and Recreation, 251 Causeway St., Suite 600, Boston, MA 02114-2104, 617/626-1250, www.mass.gov/dcr/parks/mtGreylock.

5 MOUNT GREYLOCK: DEER HILL TRAIL

2.6 mi/1.5 hr

in Mount Greylock State Reservation in Williamstown, North Adams, Adams, and Lanesborough

on Deer Hill Trail

Passing through a deep, dark grove of hemlock, this fairly easy two-mile loop leads to Deer Hill Falls, a feathering cascade of water on the upper reaches of Roaring Brook. If you have time, walk the mile from the parking area on this hike to the end of Sperry Road for excellent views from Stony Ledge of the huge glacial cirque on Greylock known as the Hopper.

From the parking area, walk or bike 0.2 mile up Sperry Road to the trailhead; stash your bike in the woods near the trailhead. the Campground Trail/Deer Hill Trail will be on the left (east). Within 0.4 mile of the trailhead, the flat, wide path crosses a brook and then comes to a right turn, descending past a grove of tall hemlocks. Just beyond, a lean-to is reached at the one-mile mark. Here, the trail descends abruptly, crosses over a stream on a wooden bridge, and then climbs steeply up to Deer Hill Falls. Another 0.2 mile above the falls, make a right turn onto the Roaring Brook Trail, which leads back to Sperry Road. Walk back 0.6 mile to the parking area at Rockwell Road.

There is a lean-to for overnight camping along the Deer Hill Trail.
User Groups: Hiker and leashed dogs. This trail is not suitable for horses; no wheelchair facilities. Bikes are prohibited.
Permits: A daily fee of $2 is collected mid-May–mid-October at some parking areas.
Maps: Find free, basic trail maps of Mount Greylock State Reservation at the park visitors center or online at the Massachusetts Division of State Parks and Recreation website. A map of area trails is available from the Appalachian Mountain Club (Northern Berkshires/Southwestern Massachusetts/Wachusett Mountain, $5.95). For topographic area maps, request North Adams and Cheshire from the USGS.
Directions: From Route 2 in Williamstown, 3.7 miles east of the junction of Routes 2 and 43, turn south onto Notch Road. Follow Notch Road up the mountain for 8.3 miles and turn right onto Rockwell Road. Continue 1.7 miles to the parking area at Sperry Road

(Sperry Road was closed to vehicle traffic in 2008). Walk or bike the road 0.2 mile to the trailhead.

From the mid-December close of hunting season through mid-May, roads within the state reservation are closed to vehicles (and groomed for snowmobiles). This trailhead is not accessible by car in winter.

GPS Coordinates: 42.6242 N, 73.1899 W

Contact: Mount Greylock State Reservation, P.O. Box 138, Rockwell Rd., Lanesborough, MA 01237, 413/499-4262 or 413/499-4263. Massachusetts Division of State Parks and Recreation, 251 Causeway St., Suite 600, Boston, MA 02114-2104, 617/626-1250, www.mass.gov/dcr/parks/mtGreylock.

⑥ MOUNT GREYLOCK: MARCH CATARACT FALLS/ STONY LEDGE

3.2 mi/1.5 hr   👣2 ⛰7

in Mount Greylock State Reservation in Williamstown, North Adams, Adams, and Lanesborough

A short, somewhat steep walk downhill from the Sperry Road Campground leads to March Cataract Falls, a 30-foot-high water curtain tumbling down the western slope of Mount Greylock. The falls are at their most magnificent in late spring and early summer; by mid-summer, it's likely that all you could find here is a gentle trickle of water.

From the parking area, walk or bike 0.6 mile to the dirt campground access road, a short half-circle that takes you to the March Cataract Falls Trail, marked by a sign. Heading east, the trail starts out on easy ground and then descends through switchbacks, reaching March Cataract Falls a mile from the campground. Though steep in sections, the trail is still suitable for kids. Head back along the same route.

Note: If the falls are just too dried up to be of any scenic value, head back to Sperry Road and walk or bike 0.5 mile north to the end of the road. Here, find Stony Ledge and matchless views of the huge glacial cirque on Greylock known as the Hopper. This detour adds an additional one mile to the round-trip, but is an easy walk on relatively flat road.

User Groups: Hikers and leashed dogs. The trail to the falls is not suitable for horses or bikes; no wheelchair facilities.

Permits: A daily fee of $2 is collected mid-May–mid-October at some parking areas.

Maps: Find free, basic trail maps of Mount Greylock State Reservation at the park visitors center or online at the Massachusetts Division of State Parks and Recreation website. A map of area trails is available from the Appalachian Mountain Club (Northern Berkshires/Southwestern Massachusetts/Wachusett Mountain, $5.95). For topographic area maps, request North Adams and Cheshire from the USGS.

Directions: From Route 2, 3.7 miles east of the junction of Routes 2 and 43 in Williamstown and 1.3 miles west of the junction of Routes 2 and 8A in North Adams, turn south onto Notch Road. Follow Notch Road up the mountain for 8.3 miles and turn right onto Rockwell Road. Continue 1.7 miles to the parking area at Sperry Road (Sperry Road closed to vehicle traffic in 2008). Walk or bike the road 0.6 mile to the dirt campground road and trailhead. Bike racks are available at the campground entrance. (This hike leaves from a trailhead only steps away from the walk-in campground off Sperry Road.)

From the mid-December close of hunting season through mid-May, roads in the state reservation are closed to vehicles (and groomed for snowmobiles). This trailhead is not accessible by car in winter.

GPS Coordinates: 42.6242 N, 73.1899 W

Contact: Mount Greylock State Reservation, P.O. Box 138, Rockwell Rd., Lanesborough, MA 01237, 413/499-4262 or 413/499-4263. Massachusetts Division of State Parks and Recreation, 251 Causeway St., Suite 600, Boston, MA 02114-2104, 617/626-1250, www.mass.gov/dcr/parks/mtGreylock.

⑦ MOUNT GREYLOCK: JONES NOSE

1 mi/0.75 hr   🏃2 ⛰8

in Mount Greylock State Reservation in Williamstown, North Adams, Adams, and Lanesborough

Jones Nose (2,552 ft.) is an open ledge on Greylock's southern ridge with broad views to the south and west all the way to the Catskill Mountains of New York State. Once an upland farm pasture and still relatively clear of forest growth, Jones Nose is a good place to catch a sunset or bring your binoculars for a fun afternoon of bird-watching. From the aery perch, you are almost certain to see hawks circling and swooping overhead, but keep an eye out for some of the northern forest dwelling birds that breed on the mountain, including swainson's thrush, yellow-rumped warbler, and dark-eyed junco.

From the parking area, walk north on the Jones Nose Trail (look for the trail marker). A well-beaten path, the trail passes through woods, crosses a meadow, and then ascends steeply to a side path on the left, a half mile from the parking lot. Follow that path 40 feet to the viewpoint. Return the way you came.

User Groups: Hikers and leashed dogs. This trail is not suitable for horses; no wheelchair facilities. Bikes are prohibited.

Permits: A daily fee of $2 is collected mid-May–mid-October at some parking areas.

Maps: Find free, basic trail maps of Mount Greylock State Reservation at the park visitors center or online at the Massachusetts Division of State Parks and Recreation website. A map of area trails is available from the Appalachian Mountain Club (Northern Berkshires/Southwestern Massachusetts/Wachusett Mountain, $5.95). For topographic area maps, request North Adams and Cheshire from the USGS.

Directions: From Route 2 in Williamstown, 3.7 miles east of the junction of Routes 2 and 43, turn south onto Notch Road. Follow Notch Road up the mountain for 8.3 miles and turn right onto Rockwell Road. Continue 3.5 miles to the Jones Nose parking lot on the left.

From the mid-December close of hunting season through mid-May, roads in the state reservation are closed to vehicles (and groomed for snowmobiles). This trailhead is not accessible by car in winter.

GPS Coordinates: 42.6014 N, 73.2007 W

Contact: Mount Greylock State Reservation, P.O. Box 138, Rockwell Rd., Lanesborough, MA 01237, 413/499-4262 or 413/499-4263. Massachusetts Division of State Parks and Recreation, 251 Causeway St., Suite 600, Boston, MA 02114-2104, 617/626-1250, www.mass.gov/dcr/parks/mtGreylock.

⑧ MOUNT GREYLOCK: ROUNDS ROCK

1 mi/0.75 hr   🏃1 ⛰9

in Mount Greylock State Reservation in Williamstown, North Adams, Adams, and Lanesborough

 BEST (

This easy one-mile loop to a pair of knobby ledges offers some of the most dramatic views to be had on Mount Greylock—and for little effort. Passing through former 1800s farmland now reforested with northern hardwoods, the short ramble through the woods leads to a sweeping vista extending south and west across the Berkshires and the Catskill Mountains. A terrific introductory hike for young children and an easy way to catch a spectacular sunset, this hike is at its best in early fall when the views burst with colorful foliage.

From the turnout, cross the road to the Rounds Rock Trail. Follow it through woods and across blueberry patches about a half mile to where a side path (at a sign that reads Scenic Vista) leads left about 75 yards to a sweeping view south from atop a low cliff. Backtrack and turn left on the main trail, following it 0.1 mile to another, shorter side path and a

© JAROSLAW TRAPSZO

a dog's eye view from the Mount Greylock summit

view south and west. Complete the loop on the Rounds Rock Trail by following it out to Rockwell Road. Turn right and walk along the road about 150 yards back to the turnout.

User Groups: Hikers and leashed dogs. This trail is not suitable for horses or skis; no wheelchair facilities. Bikes are prohibited.

Permits: A daily fee of $2 is collected mid-May–mid-October at some parking areas.

Maps: Find free, basic trail maps of Mount Greylock State Reservation at the park visitors center or online at the Massachusetts Division of State Parks and Recreation website. A map of area trails is available from the Appalachian Mountain Club (Northern Berkshires/Southwestern Massachusetts/Wachusett Mountain, $5.95). For topographic area maps, request North Adams and Cheshire from the USGS.

Directions: From Route 2 in Williamstown, 3.7 miles east of the junction of Routes 2 and 43, turn south onto Notch Road. Follow Notch Road up the mountain for 8.3 miles and turn right onto Rockwell Road. Continue 4.2 miles to a turnout on the left, across from the Rounds Rock Trail.

From the mid-December close of hunting season through mid-May, roads in the state reservation are closed to vehicles (and groomed for snowmobiles). This trailhead is not accessible by car in winter.

GPS Coordinates: 42.6014 N, 73.2007 W

Contact: Mount Greylock State Reservation, P.O. Box 138, Rockwell Rd., Lanesborough, MA 01237, 413/499-4262 or 413/499-4263. Massachusetts Division of State Parks and Recreation, 251 Causeway St., Suite 600, Boston, MA 02114-2104, 617/626-1250, www.mass.gov/dcr/parks/mtGreylock.

9 SPRUCE HILL

3 mi/1.5 hr 3 8

in Savoy Mountain State Forest near North Adams and Adams

BEST

Overshadowed by Mount Greylock to the west and the Mohawk Trail State Forest to the east, Savoy Mountain State Forest—the fourth-largest piece of Bay State public land—is also one of the state's least-known preserves. Even with 48 miles of hiking, mountain biking, and snowshoeing trails, visitor traffic is relatively low and the forest retains a rustic backwoods feel. This easy, three-mile hike provides some of the most attractive views in the region for such minimal effort; only the last stretch turns somewhat steep, and only briefly at that. Spruce Hill's summit is at 2,566 feet. The total elevation gained is about 1,200 feet.

From the parking turnout, continue for 100 feet up the forest road and turn right onto a trail signed for Spruce Hill, Hawk Lookout. Within 150 yards, the trail crosses a power line easement. About a quarter mile farther, it crosses a second set of power lines; just beyond those lines, continue straight onto the Busby Trail (marked by a sign), going uphill and following blue blazes. In a quarter mile or so, the trail crosses an old stone wall. Then, within the span of about a quarter mile, you cross a small brook, pass an old stone foundation on your right, and then pass over a stone wall. On the other side of the wall, another trail branches left, but continue straight ahead, still following the blue blazes. About 0.1 mile farther, the trail forks; both forks go to the summit, but the right option is easier and more direct, reaching the bare top of Spruce Hill within a quarter mile.

Though a few low trees grow in isolated groves on the hilltop, the summit's several open areas provide excellent views in all directions. To the west lies the Hoosic River Valley, where Route 8 runs through the towns of Adams and North Adams. Farther northwest you can see Williamstown. Across the valley rises the highest peak in Massachusetts, 3,491-foot Mount Greylock, with a prominent war memorial tower on its summit. And yes, you will see hawks. The counting station at Spruce Hill documents up to 500 birds each year, mostly seen in pairs or solitary flight. Other birds in the area include chickadees, warblers, and thrushes. Descend the way you came.

User Groups: Hikers and leashed dogs. This trail is not suitable for horses or bikes; no wheelchair facilities.

Permits: A daily parking fee of $5 is collected mid-May–mid-October.

Maps: A map of area trails is available from the Appalachian Mountain Club (Northern Berkshires/Southwestern Massachusetts/Wachusett Mountain, $5.95). For topographic area maps, request North Adams, Cheshire, and Ashfield from the USGS.

Directions: From Route 2 in Florida, 6.9 miles west of the Florida/Savoy town line and 0.4 mile east of the Florida/North Adams line, turn south onto Central Shaft Road. Continue 2.9 miles, following signs for the Savoy Mountain State Forest, to the headquarters on the right (where maps are available). Less than 0.1 mile beyond the headquarters, leave your car at the parking turnout at the start of Old Florida Road, an unmaintained woods road.

GPS Coordinates: 42.6580 N, 73.0556 W

Contact: Savoy Mountain State Forest, 260 Central Shaft Rd., Florida, MA, 01247, 413/663-8469. Massachusetts Division of State Parks and Recreation, 251 Causeway St., Suite 600, Boston, MA 02114-2104, 617/626-1250, www.mass.gov/dcr/parks/western/svym.htm.

🔟 MOHAWK TRAIL

5 mi/3.5 hr   🥾2 △7

in Mohawk Trail State Forest in Charlemont

BEST (

This mostly wooded ridge walk follows a historical route: the original Mohawk Trail, used for hundreds of years by the area's Native Americans as a connector path between the Connecticut and Hudson River Valleys. With such a storied past and still-rustic feel (parts of the route pass through a towering old-growth forest), the Mohawk Trail is a great way to bring history alive for kids. The hike ascends about 700 feet.

From the visitors center parking area, continue up the paved road, bearing left toward the camping area where the road forks, then bearing right at a sign for the Indian Trail

© JAROSLAW TRAPSZO

a birch-lined trail in the Mohawk Trail State Forest, Charlemont

at 0.7 mile. The trail remains flat for only about 200 feet, then turns right, and begins the steep and relentless ascent for a half mile to the ridge. This trail is not well marked and can be easy to lose in a few places. Once atop the ridge, the walking grows much easier and you will quickly reach a well-marked trail junction. Here, turn right onto the Todd Mountain Trail, following it a half mile to an open ledge with a good view overlooking the Cold River Valley. Double back to the trail junction and this time, continue straight ahead on the Clark Mountain Trail; you will see disks on trees indicating that this is the old Mohawk Trail. The easy, wide path predates European settlement here by hundreds of years. About 0.8 mile past the trail junction, the Clark Mountain/Mohawk Trail swings right and begins descending; double back from here to the junction and descend the Indian Trail back to the start.

User Groups: Hikers and leashed dogs. This trail is not suitable for bikes or horses; no wheelchair facilities.

Permits: A daily parking fee of $5 is collected mid-May–mid-October.

Maps: A free, basic trail and contour map of Mohawk Trail State Forest is available at the state forest headquarters or at the Massachusetts Division of State Parks and Recreation website. For a topographic area map, request Rowe from the USGS.

Directions: From the junction of Routes 2 and 8A in Charlemont, follow Route 2 west for 3.7 miles to the state forest entrance road on the right. Drive the state forest road for 0.2 mile, through a gate, and park just beyond the gate on the left, behind the headquarters building.

GPS Coordinates: 42.6430 N, 72.9464 W

Contact: Mohawk Trail State Forest, P.O. Box 7, Rte. 2, Charlemont, MA 01339, 413/339-5504. Massachusetts Division of State Parks and Recreation, 251 Causeway St., Suite 600, Boston, MA 02114-2104, 617/626-1250, www.mass.gov/dcr/parks/western/mhwk.htm.

11 GIANT TREES OF CLARK RIDGE

1.5 mi/1 hr   🥾4 ⛰️8

in Mohawk Trail State Forest in Charlemont

The steep, rugged terrain you encounter on the north flank of Clark Ridge is probably a big part of the reason loggers left so many giant trees untouched here over the past few centuries—a time period during which most of New England was deforested. Within an area of about 75 acres are an uncounted number of sugar maple, red oak, white ash, beech, and other hardwoods reaching more than 120 feet into the sky, and aged 200–300 years. One respected regional expert has identified a 160-foot white pine here as the tallest living thing in New England. Walking around in this cathedral of bark is a rare and stirring experience. And unlike other hikes in this book, this one doesn't follow an established trail. It begins on an abandoned, somewhat overgrown logging road and becomes a bushwhack through the woods.

From either parking area near the Zoar picnic area, walk across the bridge and immediately turn left, following a faint footpath down across a wash and a cleared area and onto a distinct trail—actually an abandoned logging road. The road dissipates within about a half mile, but you need only to continue walking a quarter mile, then turn right, and bushwhack uphill on the ridge to find the tall trees—there is no mistaking it when you get there. Other bushwhackers before you may have already carved out a pretty recognizable trail, but this is still off-grid hiking; bring a compass, be sure to remember how to find your way back to the logging road, and allow extra time for taking in the wild beauty of this ancient forest.

User Groups: Hikers and leashed dogs. This trail is not suitable for bikes or horses; no wheelchair facilities.

Permits: A daily parking fee of $5 is collected mid-May–mid-October.

Maps: There is no trail map for this hike, but a free, basic map of the Mohawk Trail State Forest is available at the state forest headquarters or at the Massachusetts Division of State Parks and Recreation website. For a topographic area map, request Rowe from the USGS.

Directions: From the junction of Routes 2 and 8A in Charlemont, follow Route 2 for 1.6 miles to a right turn at the Rowe/Monroe sign. Proceed 2.2 miles, bear left, and continue another 0.8 mile to the Zoar picnic area on the left, where there is parking, or to parking 0.1 mile farther on the right, immediately before the bridge over Deerfield River.

GPS Coordinates: 42.6523 N, 72.9514 W

Contact: Mohawk Trail State Forest, P.O. Box 7, Rte. 2, Charlemont, MA 01339, 413/339-5504. Massachusetts Division of State Parks and Recreation, 251 Causeway St., Suite 600, Boston, MA 02114-2104, 617/626-1250, www.mass.gov/dcr/parks/western/mhwk.htm.

12 THE LOOKOUT
2.2 mi/1.5 hr

in Mohawk Trail State Forest in Charlemont

Here's an easy 2.2-mile walk through the tranquil woods of Mohawk Trail State Forest to a lookout with a good view east toward the pastoral Deerfield River Valley and Charlemont. Without any real rugged footing to be weary of, it's a great opportunity to spot squirrels, rabbits, and deer darting to and fro along the trail. Even ruffled grouse are seen in the area, but stay quiet when you spot one—the woodland birds often explode into flight and beat their wings very loudly when surprised.

From the parking turnout and picnic area, cross the road to the Totem Trail, which begins behind a stone marker for the state forest. The trail is obvious and well marked, crossing a small brook and reaching the overlook in 1.1 miles. Hike back along the same route. This hike climbs about 600 feet.

User Groups: Hikers and leashed dogs. The trail is not suitable for bikes or horses; no wheelchair facilities.

Permits: A daily parking fee of $5 is collected mid-May–mid-October.

Maps: A free, basic trail and contour map of Mohawk Trail State Forest is available at the state forest headquarters or at the Massachusetts Division of State Parks and Recreation website. For a topographic area map, request Rowe from the USGS.

Directions: From the junction of Routes 2 and 8A in Charlemont, follow Route 2 west for 4.6 miles to a parking turnout and picnic area (0.9 mile west of the Mohawk Trail State Forest's main entrance).

GPS Coordinates: 42.6420 N, 72.9476 W

Contact: Mohawk Trail State Forest, P.O. Box 7, Rte. 2, Charlemont, MA 01339, 413/339-5504. Massachusetts Division of State Parks and Recreation, 251 Causeway St., Suite 600, Boston, MA 02114-2104, 617/626-1250, www.mass.gov/dcr/parks/western/mhwk.htm.

13 FIRE TOWER HIKE
3 mi/1.5 hr   🏃2 ▲7

in D.A.R. State Forest in Goshen

A winding walk through the 1,800-acre
D.A.R. State Forest, a tract of former farmland donated to the state by the Daughters of
the American Revolution (D.A.R.), this hike
passes through lush woodlands on the way to
panoramic views from the state forest's fire
tower. Out and back, the total elevation gain
on this trek is a modest 250 feet.

From the parking area at Moore Hill Road,
this hike begins between the boat launch and
the night registration office and follows the
Long Trail (not to be confused with the trail
running the length of Vermont). The path is
well marked as it twists and turns its way 1.5
miles through the forest to reach the fire tower
atop Moore's Hill (1,697 ft.). Climbing the
tower's steps, views of the surrounding countryside stretch all the way northeast to New
Hampshire's Mount Monadnock, southeast
to the Holyoke Range and Mount Tom, and
northwest to Mount Greylock. Descend the
same way you hiked up.

User Groups: Hikers and leashed dogs. This
trail is not suitable for bikes or horses; no
wheelchair facilities.

Permits: A daily parking fee of $5 is collected
mid-May–mid-October.

Maps: A free trail map is available at the state
forest or at the Massachusetts Division of State
Parks and Recreation website. For topographic
area maps, request Holyoke from the USGS.

Directions: From North Main Street in
Northampton, follow Route 9 west for 12
miles to Goshen. Turn right onto Cape Street/
Route 112 north and continue for 0.7 mile.
The park entrance is on the right at Moore
Hill Road. In summer, park in the second
lot along Moore Hill Road, located just past
the left turn for the boat launch and nature
center. In winter, park in the first lot, near the
restrooms and warming hut (Moore Hill Road
is not maintained beyond that point).

GPS Coordinates: 42.4569 N, 72.7917 W
Contact: D.A.R. State Forest, Rte. 112, Goshen, MA, 413/268-7098; or mail to 555 East
St., RFD 1, Williamsburg, MA 01096. Massachusetts Division of State Parks and Recreation, 251 Causeway St., Suite 600, Boston,
MA 02114-2104, 617/626-1250, www.mass.
gov/dcr/parks/western/darf.htm.

14 BALANCING ROCK
1 mi/0.75 hr   🏃2 ▲7

in D.A.R. State Forest in Goshen

Here is a hike of about one mile that is both
worthwhile and easy—even for young children—leading to the "balancing rock," a grav-
ity defying glacial erratic set in the middle of
a beautiful deciduous forest (a blazing sight
for the eyes in autumn). Other erratics are
tucked away along the trail, all dumped here
thousands of years ago by melting Ice Age
glaciers.

From the summer parking lot along Moore
Hill Road, cross the road to head south along
the blue-blazed woods road. At the intersection of several trails, turn left onto the trail
with orange blazes and follow it all the way
to Balancing Rock, a truck-size boulder in
the woods. Continue on the orange-blazed
trail past Balancing Rock, paralleling a stone
wall at one point and then ducking into deep
woods for a short loop back to the multi-trail
junction. Reaching the junction, turn left on
the blue-blazed trail and return to the parking lot.

User Groups: Hikers and leashed dogs. No
horses, bikes, or wheelchair facilities.

Permits: A daily parking fee of $5 is collected
mid-May–mid-October.

Maps: A free trail map is available at the state
forest or at the Massachusetts Division of State
Parks and Recreation website.

Directions: From North Main Street in
Northampton, follow Route 9 west for 12
miles to Goshen. Turn right onto Cape Street/

Route 112 north and continue for 0.7 mile. The park entrance is on the right at Moore Hill Road. In summer, park in the second lot along Moore Hill Road, located just past the left turn for the boat launch and nature center. In winter, park in the first lot, near the restrooms and warming hut (Moore Hill Road is not maintained beyond that point).
GPS Coordinates: 42.4569 N, 72.7917 W
Contact: D.A.R. State Forest, Rte. 112, Goshen, MA, 413/268-7098; or mail to 555 East St., RFD 1, Williamsburg, MA 01096. Massachusetts Division of State Parks and Recreation, 251 Causeway St., Suite 600, Boston, MA 02114-2104, 617/626-1250, www.mass.gov/dcr/parks/western/darf.htm.

15 SOUTH SUGARLOAF MOUNTAIN
1.5 mi/1 hr 2 8

in Mount Sugarloaf State Reservation in South Deerfield

At just 652 feet above sea level, South Sugarloaf is barely a hill. But as it rises abruptly from the flat valley, its cliffs loom surprisingly high over the wide Connecticut River and surrounding landscape of town, farmland, and forest. Reached via a short but steep hike, the South Sugarloaf summit offers some of the Bay State's best views of the Connecticut Valley's quaint tableau. The vertical ascent of the hike is about 300 feet.

From the parking lot, the wide (though unmarked) West Side Trail leads into the woods. Take the West Side Trail only a very short distance before leaving on the side trail branching to the right. This trail leads across the Summit Road to the start of the Pocumtuck Ridge Trail, marked by a wooden post without a sign. (The Pocumtuck Ridge Trail can also be reached by walking up the Summit Road about 100 feet inside the gate.) Follow the Pocumtuck's blue blazes straight up the steep hillside under power lines; the trail finally makes several switchbacks just below the summit ledges. As the sweeping vista comes in to view from atop the cliffs, continue on to the summit's observation tower for even longer views of the surrounding countryside. Return the same way.
User Groups: Hikers and leashed dogs. This trail is not suitable for bikes or horses; no wheelchair facilities.

view from South Sugarloaf Mountain

Permits: A daily parking fee of $2 is collected mid-May–mid-October.

Maps: For a free, basic map of hiking trails, contact the Mount Sugarloaf State Reservation or see the Massachusetts Division of State Parks and Recreation website. For a topographic area map, request Williamsburg from the USGS.

Directions: From the junction of Routes 47 and 116 in Sunderland, drive 0.7 mile west on Route 116 and turn right onto Sugarloaf Road. The Mount Sugarloaf State Reservation Summit Road begins immediately on the right; park in the dirt lot along Sugarloaf Road just beyond the turn for the Summit Road.

GPS Coordinates: 42.4675 N, 72.5945 W

Contact: Mount Sugarloaf State Reservation, Sugarloaf St./Rte. 116, South Deerfield, MA 01373, 413/545-5993. Massachusetts Division of State Parks and Recreation, 251 Causeway St., Suite 600, Boston, MA 02114-2104, 617/626-1250, www.mass.gov/dcr/parks/central/msug.htm.

🔢 MOUNT TOBY
5 mi/3.5 hr   🥾5 ⛰7

in Sunderland

Mount Toby's 1,269-foot summit is wooded, but a fire tower open to the public offers panoramic views stretching up to 50 miles across five states when the weather is clear. The well-maintained Summit Road provides a route to the top that can be hiked easily—or biked or skied by anyone seeking a fairly challenging climb and a fast descent. The hike described here ascends the Summit Road but descends the steeper Telephone Line Trail, a net climb of 800 feet.

The Summit Road begins behind the Mount Toby Forest sign, with frequent white blazes on the route beginning a short distance down the road. After less than a mile, the Telephone Line Trail (which you'll follow on the descent) diverges right. Approaching

the summit at almost two miles, the road coincides with the orange-blazed Robert Frost Trail to reach the top. From the fire tower at the top, follow the marked Telephone Line Trail for the descent off Mount Toby. The Telephone Line Trail eventually reaches the Summit Road near the start of the hike; turn left and follow the Summit Road back to the trailhead. Another option for the return trip is to pick up the Robert Frost Trail, which diverges left about halfway down the Telephone Line Trail and also leads back to the Summit Road start.

User Groups: Hikers and leashed dogs. The Summit Road is suitable for bikes and horses; no wheelchair facilities.

Permits: Mount Toby Reservation is owned by the University of Massachusetts, but is open for public use. Parking and access are free.

Maps: The Mount Toby Reservation Trail Map is $3.95 from New England Cartographics, 413/549-4124 or toll-free 888/995-6277, www.necartographics.com. For topographic area maps, request Greenfield and Williamsburg from the USGS.

Directions: From the junction of Routes 47 and 63 in Sunderland, follow Route 47 south for 0.9 mile to a left turn onto Reservation Road. Follow the road for a half mile and park in a dirt lot on the right, just past the sign for the Mount Toby Forest.

GPS Coordinates: 42.5037 N, 72.5311 W

Contact: University of Massachusetts, Natural Resources Conservation, 160 Holdsworth Way, Amherst, MA 01003-9285, 413/545-2665.

🔢 PITTSFIELD STATE FOREST: TRANQUILITY TRAIL
1.5 mi/1 hr   🥾1 ⛰7

in Pittsfield

BEST (

Sitting almost directly on the Taconic Range ridgeline, Pittsfield State Forest is a sprawling

10,000-acre tract of woods, hills, ponds, streams, and over 65 acres of azaleas—a big tourist draw in June when the flowering shrubs burst into bloom. The paved three-quarter mile long Tranquility Trail is popular with wheelchair hikers and other visitors who favor a smooth walking surface. A quiet woodland ramble right in the middle of one of the Berkshire's most popular recreation areas, this satisfying hike really lives up to its name. Other universal access amenities in the state forest include a wheelchair-accessible picnic and restroom, both located very close to the trailhead.

The well-marked Tranquility Trail begins next to the ski area parking lot. Crossing a wheelchair-accessible bridge just steps from the trailhead, the paved path then winds along under a canopy of mixed forest cover to reach its end at a picturesque pond. Along the route, you will probably spot some of the region's more common animal inhabitants—salamanders, turtles, and garter snakes are often fellow travelers along the path and wild turkey, fox, deer, porcupines, and weasel can sometimes be seen lurking among the trees. To learn more about the flora and fauna of the Tranquility Trail, interpretive audio tapes are available from the forest headquarters (near the entrance gate). Return the way you came.

User Groups: Hikers, wheelchairs, bikes, horses, and leashed dogs.

Permits: A $5 day-use fee per vehicle is charged early-May–mid-October. Parking is free for ParksPass holders, vehicles with Handicapped, POW, and disabled veteran plates/placard, and seniors 62 and above with the Massachusetts Senior Pass.

Maps: A basic trail map for Pittsfield State Forest is available at the park entrance. For a topographic map of area trails, request the Pittsfield quad from the USGS.

Directions: From downtown Pittsfield, head south on North Street to a right turn on U.S. 20 west. Follow U.S. 20 for 2.2 miles and then take a right turn onto Hungerford Avenue;

continue for 0.2 mile, then bear left onto Fort Hill Avenue and continue for 1 mile. Turn left onto West Street. Continue for 0.2 mile, and turn right onto Churchill Street and continue for 1.7 miles to Cascade Street. Turn left and follow the brown lead-in signs to the park. From the park entrance, follow the access road a short distance to the ski area. The Tranquility Trail begins at the handicap-accessible parking lot on the left. The forest is open sunrise–8 P.M. year-round.

GPS Coordinates: 42.4895 N, 73.2995 W

Contact: Pittsfield State Forest, 1041 Cascade St., Pittsfield, MA 01201, 413/442-8992, www.mass.gov/dcr/parks/western/pitt.htm. Universal Access Program, Massachusetts Department of Conservation and Recreation, P.O. Box 484, Amherst, MA 01004, 413/545-5353 (voice), 413/577-2200 (TTY), www.mass.gov/dcr/universal_access.

🔢18 PLEASANT VALLEY WILDLIFE SANCTUARY: BEAVER LOOP
1.6 mi/1 hr 🚶1 ⛰8

in Lenox

The Berkshires' outpost of the Massachusetts Audubon Society, Pleasant Valley Wildlife Sanctuary is a network of ponds, meadows, marshes, and upland forest at the foot of Lenox Mountain. Known for its enormous beaver population, the sanctuary is also home to a variety or waterfowl and wood warblers and is a nesting ground for the common yellowthroat. This easy loop takes you through the variety of ecosystems found within the sanctuary and offers the best chance for wildlife-viewing. Trails within the sanctuary are clearly signed and marked with two sets of blazes: blue blazes on the trail indicate you are moving away from the office and nature center; yellow blazes mean you are returning to the office.

From the parking area near the sanctuary office, follow the gravel path to the nature center, passing a bee balm and wildflower garden filled with fluttering hummingbirds and butterflies. At the center, pick up the Blue Bird Trail and follow briefly to a trail junction. Here, turn right on the Alexander Trail and enter a hardwood forest of linden, black birch, and ash. At 0.3 mile from the office, reach another trail junction. Turn right on the Yokun Trail and then turn left on a short loop path that edges along a marshy beaver pond. Turn left again once you return to the Yokun Trail and follow 0.5 mile to a left turn onto the Old Woods Road. Crossing over two brooks, the wide, forest-covered path ambles along to a junction with the Beaver Trail. Turn left on the Beaver Trail and wander along the edge of Beaver Pond, taking in what can only be described as a beaver's version of urban sprawl: Dams are everywhere. Also living here are muskrats, similar in appearance to beavers, except for their rat-like tails. At one mile, leave the pond and turn left on the Bluebird Trail, a downhill jaunt through hemlock woods. At 1.3 miles, turn right on the Yokun Trail, skirting two shallow ponds, a favorite haunt of local waterfowl, including heron, mallards, and Canada geese. At 1.6 miles, the trail circles back to the office, crossing a broad swamp before returning to the parking area.

User Groups: Hikers only. No bikes, dogs, or horses. There are no wheelchair facilities on this hike; the sanctuary's All People Trail, nature center, and all restroom facilities do offer universal access.

Permits: Trails open dawn–dusk on the days the Pleasant Valley nature center is open. Access costs are $4 for nonmember adults and $3 for nonmember children (ages 2–12) and seniors.

Maps: A sanctuary trail map is available at the Pleasant Valley nature center.

Directions: From the center of Lenox, follow U.S. 7A north to an intersection with U.S. 7/U.S. 20; turn left and continue approximately one mile to a left turn onto West Dugway Road. The sanctuary and parking area are 1.6

miles ahead on the right. Nature center hours: Tuesday–Friday 9 A.M.–5 P.M.; Saturday, Sunday, and Monday holidays, 10 A.M.–4 P.M. GPS Coordinates: 42.3852 N, 73.2969 W

Contact: Pleasant Valley Audubon Wildlife Sanctuary, 472 West Mountain Rd., Lenox, MA 01240, 413/637-0320, www.massaudubon.org/Nature_Connection/Sanctuaries/Pleasant_Valley.

19 PLEASANT VALLEY WILDLIFE SANCTUARY: LENOX MOUNTAIN
2 mi/1.5 hr   🏃3 ⛰8

in Lenox

Lenox Mountain is a popular hike for summer visitors to Lenox. A few hikers (with either super human hearing or a very good imagination) claim music from nearby Tanglewood can be heard from the mountain's lofty heights. Whether you hear nature sounds or a few stray notes of Mozart as you make your way up the short, moderately strenuous trek to the top of 2,126-foot Lenox Mountain, the fire tower lookout at the summit offers a symphony of views extending to the surrounding Berkshire hills and even west into New York State. This out-and-back hike starts and finishes at the Massachusetts Audubon Society's Pleasant Valley Wildlife Sanctuary, a refuge nestled at the foot of Lenox Mountain that is known for its large beaver populations. The Overlook Trail climb nets an elevation gain of 800 feet.

From the parking area near the sanctuary office, follow the gravel path to the nature center. At the center, pick up the Blue Bird Trail and follow briefly, crossing through a field and over a brook before reaching a well-marked trail junction. Here, turn left on the Overlook Trail and follow the blue blazes up the rapidly steepening trail. (Blue blazes mark the trail up and indicate you are moving away from the office; on the descent, yellow blazes on the other side of the trees indicate you are headed towards the office.) In about one mile, the mountain's open summit is reached. Enhance your views by climbing the fire tower. Take in the breathtaking landscape or look to the sky to spot hawks and even the occasional bald eagle. Return the way you came, following the yellow blazes back to the parking area.

User Groups: Hikers only. No bikes, dogs, or horses. There are no wheelchair facilities on this hike; the sanctuary's All People Trail, nature center, and all restroom facilities do offer universal access.

Permits: Trails open dawn–dusk on the days the Pleasant Valley nature center is open. Access costs are $4 for nonmember adults and $3 for nonmember children (ages 2–12) and seniors.

Maps: A sanctuary trail map is available at the Pleasant Valley nature center.

Directions: From the center of Lenox, follow U.S. 7A north to an intersection with U.S. 7/U.S. 20; turn left and continue approximately one mile to a left turn onto West Dugway Road. The sanctuary and parking area are 1.6 miles ahead on the right. Nature center hours: Tuesday–Friday 9 A.M.–5 P.M.; Saturday, Sunday, and Monday holidays, 10 A.M.–4 P.M. GPS Coordinates: 42.3852 N, 73.2969 W

Contact: Pleasant Valley Audubon Wildlife Sanctuary, 472 West Mountain Rd., Lenox, MA 01240, 413/637-0320, www.massaudubon.org/Nature_Connection/Sanctuaries/Pleasant_Valley.

20 MONUMENT MOUNTAIN
1.6 mi/1 hr   🚶2 ⛰10

in Great Barrington

BEST (

A fine trek that rivals even the Mount Greylock region for the best hiking in southern New England, Monument Mountain is an unmistakable gray-white quartzite ridge thrust high above the surrounding landscape. Its summit, Squaw Peak, rises to 1,640 feet and offers three-state views in all directions. Arguably even more dramatic, though, are the cliffs south of Squaw Peak and the detached rock pinnacle known as Devil's Pulpit. A good time to come here is mid-June, when the mountain laurel blooms, or late September when the surrounding hills turn crimson and gold. This unique hill has been popular since at least the 19th century: In 1850, so legend goes, Nathaniel Hawthorne, Oliver Wendell Holmes, and Herman Melville picnicked together on Monument's summit. And William Cullen Bryant wrote a poem titled "Monument Mountain" relating the tale of a Mahican maiden who, spurned in love, leapt to her death from the cliffs. Your hike may be less historic and less traumatic than either of those, but Monument Mountain is one not to miss.

This fairly easy, 1.6-mile hike ascends and descends the Hickey Trail, but you may enjoy making a loop hike, going up the Hickey and coming down the 1.3-mile Indian Monument Trail, which joins up with the Hickey below the summit. At the picnic area, a sign describes the trail heading south, the Indian Monument Trail, as easier, and the Hickey Trail, which heads north, as steeper. The Hickey actually grows steep for only a short section below the summit and is otherwise a well-graded and well-maintained trail. Following the Hickey's white blazes, you parallel a brook with a small waterfall. Nearing the summit ridge, watch for a trail entering on the right; that's the Indian Monument Trail, and you want to be able to distinguish it from the Hickey on your way back down. From the summit, continue following the white blazes south about a quarter mile, passing a pile of rocks, until you reach the cliffs. Devil's Pulpit is the obvious pinnacle at the far end of the cliffs. Return the way you came or take the Indian Monument Trail.

User Groups: Hikers and leashed dogs. No wheelchair facilities. Bikes and horses are prohibited.

Permits: Parking and access are free. On-site donations welcome.

Maps: A map of trails is posted on an information board at the picnic area and a paper map is available at the trailhead. A map is also available from The Trustees of Reservations. For topographic area maps, request Great Barrington and Stockbridge from the USGS.

Directions: From intersection of U.S 7 and Route 102 at the Red Lion Inn in Stockbridge center, take U.S. 7 south and follow for three miles; entrance and parking are on the right. From Great Barrington, take U.S. 7 north for four miles to entrance and parking (room for 56 cars) on left. Monument Mountain is open to the public sunrise–sunset year-round.

GPS Coordinates: 42.2468 N, 73.3325 W

Contact: The Trustees of Reservations Western Management Region, Mission House, P.O. Box 792, Sergeant St., Stockbridge, MA 01262-0792, 413/298-3239, www.thetrustees.org.

21 ICE GLEN AND LAURA'S TOWER LOOP
3.3 mi/2 hr   🥾2 ⛰8

in Stockbridge

Not far from Stockbridge's quaint village center is the Ice Glen, a boulder strewn ravine popular with hikers in spring when meltwaters refreeze on the rocks to form a sparkling fairyland of temporary ice sculptures. For summer visitors to Stockbridge, the moss-covered glen provides a cool escape from the heat and from the area's tourist crowds. This easy loop hike takes you first on a gentle climb to Laura's Tower, a picturesque overlook with excellent views of Stockbridge. Expect an elevation gain of approximately 650 feet on this pleasant trek.

From the parking circle, pick up the white-blazed Ice Glen Trail at a large marker and trail map. Only a few steps into this hike, a suspension bridge takes you over the Housatonic River; the trail then crosses railroad tracks, passes under power lines, and enters the woods within the first 0.25 mile. Next, when you reach a trail junction, bear left onto the orange-blazed Laura's Tower Trail. Follow the path 0.7 mile to an observation tower; climbing up on the open platform reveals postcard perfect views of Stockbridge's historic village center. Retracing your steps back to the trail junction, take a left on the Ice Glen Trail and in another 0.3 mile, enter the ravine's rocky maze. Pay attention to footing as the trail picks its way along often slippery moss-covered boulders. After 0.4 mile, the trail leaves the ravine and reenters the woods (look here for a very tall pine tree, reportedly the tallest one in Massachusetts). In 0.1 mile, the trail passes a private driveway and continues straight to reach Ice Glen Road. Turn right and follow the road 0.5 mile back to U.S. 7. Turn right again and follow U.S. 7 for 0.3 mile to a right turn onto Park Street. From here, it's only a short distance to the parking circle.

User Groups: Hikers only. This trail is not suitable for bikes, dogs, or horses; no wheelchair facilities.

Permits: Parking and access are free.

Maps: A free trail map is available from the Laurel Hill Association, the village improvement society in charge of maintaining the trails. For a topographic area map, request Stockbridge from the USGS.

Directions: From the center of Stockbridge, drive south 0.2 mile on U.S. 7 to a left turn onto Park Street. Drive 0.3 mile to the road's end and parking circle.

GPS Coordinates: 42.2782 N, 73.3076 W

Contact: Laurel Hill Association - Trails, P.O. Box 24, Stockbridge, MA 01262.

22 BENEDICT POND AND THE LEDGES
2.5 mi/1.5 hr   🥾2 ⛰8

in Beartown State Forest in Monterey

BEST (

An easy loop around pristine Benedict Pond, this hike takes you to a place simply teaming with critters: hear the tap, tap, tapping of woodpeckers; see beavers hard at work; watch mallards and Canada geese take flight across the water; and catch sight of frogs and toads patiently awaiting their next meal. The loop also leads to the Ledges, a stop on the Appalachian Trail with excellent views west towards East Mountain and Mount Everett. Kids love this nature trek, a net climb of only a few hundred feet.

From the parking area, follow the blue-blazed Pond Loop Trail as it edges along the water to the pond's eastern end. Here, the trail merges with the white-blazed Appalachian Trail (AT). Turn left. The coinciding trails soon reach a woods road and split again. Turn right onto the AT, ascending a low hillside. Where the AT hooks right and crosses a brook, continue straight ahead on a short side path to an impressive beaver dam that has flooded a swamp. Backtrack, cross the brook on the AT, and within several minutes you reach the Ledges, with a view west toward East Mountain and Mount Everett. Backtrack on the AT to the woods road and turn right onto the Pond Loop Trail. Watch for where the trail bears left off the woods road (at a sign and blue blazes). The trail passes through the state forest campground on the way back to the parking area.

User Groups: Hikers and leashed dogs. Bikes and horses are prohibited; no wheelchair facilities.

Permits: A daily parking fee of $5 is collected mid-May–mid-October.

Maps: A contour map of trails (designating uses allowed on each trail) is available in boxes at the state forest headquarters, at the trailhead parking area, at a trail information kiosk at the swimming area and restrooms, and at the campground. You can also find one at the Massachusetts Division of State Parks and Recreation website. A map of area trails is available from the Appalachian Mountain Club (Blue Hills, Mount Tom, Mount Holyoke, $6.95). For topographic area maps, request Great Barrington and Otis from the USGS.

Directions: From the Monterey General Store

in Monterey, follow Route 23 for 2.4 miles west to a left turn on Blue Hill (signs are posted for Beartown State Forest). Follow Blue Hill Road 0.7 mile to the forest headquarters on the left. Continuing north on Blue Hill Road, you pass the Appalachian Trail crossing 1.3 miles from the headquarters; at 1.5 miles, turn right onto Benedict Pond Road (shown as Beartown Road on the park map). Follow signs to the Pond Loop Trail; the trailhead leaves from a dirt parking area. A short distance farther up the road are public restrooms and a state forest campground. Beartown State Forest is closed from dusk to a half hour before sunrise year-round.

GPS Coordinates: 42.2023 N, 73.2889 W

Contact: Beartown State Forest, Blue Hill Rd., P.O. Box 97, Monterey, MA 01245-0097, 413/528-0904. Massachusetts Division of State Parks and Recreation, 251 Causeway St., Suite 600, Boston, MA 02114-2104, 617/626-1250, www.mass.gov/dcr/parks/western/bear.htm.

23 NORWOTTUCK TRAIL
10.1 mi one-way/5 hr

in Northampton

The 10.1-mile-long Norwottuck Trail is a paved bike path that follows a former railroad bed from Northampton, crossing over the Connecticut River and passing through Hadley and Amherst, on its way into Belchertown. The trail's flat course provides a linear, universally accessible recreation area for walkers, runners, bicyclists, in-line skaters, and wheelchairs. Historians believe that the Native Americans who lived here before the European settlers were called the Norwottucks. Translated, norwottuck means "in the midst of the river," the Native American term for the entire Connecticut River Valley. As with any bike or pedestrian path, the Norwottuck is popular with families because it provides a refuge from traffic. The place from which many users access the trail is the large parking lot at its western end; this lot is often full, so it's wise to try one of the other access points listed in the directions.

User Groups: Hikers, bikers, dogs, and wheelchair users. Dogs must be leashed. Horses are prohibited.

Permits: Parking and access are free.

Maps: A brochure/map is available at both trailheads. The Western Massachusetts Bicycle Map, a detailed bicycling map covering the state from the New York border to the Quabbin Reservoir, including the Norwottuck Trail, is available for $4.25 from Rubel BikeMaps (P.O. Box 401035, Cambridge, MA 02140, 617/776-6567, www.bikemaps.com) and from area stores listed at the website. For topographic area maps, request Easthampton and Holyoke from the USGS.

Directions: To reach the trail's western end from the south, take I-91 to Exit 19 in Northampton. Down the off-ramp, drive straight through the intersection and turn right into the Connecticut River Greenway State Park/Elwell Recreation Area. From the north, take I-91 to Exit 20 in Northampton. Turn left at the traffic lights and drive 1.5 miles to the Elwell Recreation Area on the left. The trail can also be accessed from four other parking areas: behind the Whole Foods store in the Mountain Farms Mall on Route 9 in Hadley, 3.7 miles from the Elwell Recreation Area parking lot; near the junction of Mill Lane and Southeast Street, off Route 9 in Amherst; on Station Road in Amherst (reached via Southeast Street off Route 9), 1.6 miles from the trail's eastern terminus; and on Warren Wright Road in Belchertown, the trail's eastern terminus. Public restrooms are available at the parking area at Elwell Recreation Area. GPS Coordinates: 42.3350 N, 72.6220 W

Contact: Connecticut River Greenway State Park/Elwell Recreation Area, 136 Damon Rd., Northampton, MA 01060, 413/586-8706, ext. 12. Massachusetts Division of State Parks and Recreation, 251 Causeway St., Suite 600, Boston, MA 02114-2104, 617/626-1250, www.mass.gov/dcr/parks/central/nwrt.htm.

24 MOUNT TOM
5.4 mi/2.5 hr 👫4 △8

in Mount Tom State Reservation in Holyoke

BEST (

One of the most popular stretches of the 98-mile Metacomet-Monadnock Trail is this traverse of the Mount Tom Ridge. A steep mountainside capped by tall basalt cliffs defines Mount Tom's west face and the trail follows the brink of that precipice for nearly two miles, treating hikers to commanding views west as far as the Berkshires on a clear day. Mount Tom is also one of New England's premier sites for spotting migrating hawks. Each fall, thousands of hawks and other birds fly past the mountain on their way south. For all the incredible scenery, this hike climbs less than 500 feet.

From the parking area, walk up the paved Smiths Ferry Road for about 75 yards to reach the reservation's interpretative center (located in a stone house). Turn right at the house and enter the woods; the trail is marked by white rectangular blazes and a triangular marker for the Metacomet-Monadnock Trail. Within minutes, the trail veers right and climbs steeply toward Goat Peak. Pass a good view westward and then reach the open clearing of Goat Peak, where the lookout tower offers pleasing panoramic views. Double back to Smiths Ferry Road, turn right, walk about 75 yards, and then enter the woods on the left, following the white blazes of the Metacomet-Monadnock Trail. It crosses the Quarry Trail and then ascends the ridge. Numerous side paths lead to the right to great views from the cliffs, with each view better than the last, until you reach the Mount Tom summit, where there are radio and television transmission stations. Take in the sights again as you retrace your steps on the Metacomet-Monadnock Trail to your car.

User Groups: Hikers and leashed dogs. Bikes and horses are prohibited; no wheelchair facilities.

Permits: A daily parking fee of $2 is collected mid-May–mid-October.

Maps: A free map of hiking trails is available at the reservation headquarters and the stone house, or at the Massachusetts Division of State Parks and Recreation website. A map of area trails is available from the Appalachian Mountain Club (Blue Hills Reservation/ Mount Tom/Holyoke Range, $6.95). For topographic area maps, request Mount Tom, Easthampton, Mount Holyoke, and Spring-field North from the USGS.

Directions: From I-91, take Exit 18 (East-hampton/Holyoke)to U.S. 5 south. Follow U.S. 5 south for roughly 3.3 miles to a right turn onto Smiths Ferry Road, at the entrance to Mount Tom State Reservation. Follow the road for nearly a mile, passing under I-91 to a horseshoe-shaped parking area on the right. The parking area is about 0.2 mile before the reservation's interpretive center.

GPS Coordinates: 42.2680 N, 72.6320 W

Contact: Mount Tom State Reservation, 125 Reservation Rd., U.S. 5, Holyoke, MA 01040, 413/534-1186. Massachusetts Division of State Parks and Recreation, 251 Causeway St., Suite 600, Boston, MA 02114-2104, 617/626-1250, www.mass.gov/dcr/parks/central/mtom. htm.

25 JUG END
2.2 mi/1 hr   🏃3 ⛰8

in Egremont

No, the summit of Jug End (1,770 ft.) looks nothing like a handle, base, or spout of a jug. The name comes from a rather poor English translation of the Dutch and German word for youth, *jugend,* as early Dutch settlers in the area were called. However you pronounce it, the views from the cliffs and open ledges on Jug End are well worth the short, if steep, hike of more than 500 feet uphill.

From the turnout, follow the white blazes of the Appalachian Trail in an instantly steep uphill trudge. Within 0.3 mile, the trail ascends the ridge, reaching the first open views

at about 0.7 mile from the road. Continuing on, Jug End's summit is soon reached at 1.1 miles from the road. Good views northward toward the pastoral valley and the surrounding hills of the southern Berkshires are especially spectacular in early autumn. After you've taken in the views, head back to the parking area the same way you hiked up. This is a sharp descent that can be hard on the knees.

User Groups: Hikers and leashed dogs. Trail is not suitable for bikes or horses; no wheelchair facilities.

Permits: Parking and access are free.

Maps: A free map of hiking trails is available from the reservation headquarters or at the Massachusetts Division of State Parks and Recreation website. For topographic area maps, request Ashley Falls and Great Bar-rington from the USGS.

Directions: From the junction of Routes 23 and 41 in Egremont, drive south on Route 41 for 0.1 mile and turn right onto Mount Washington Road. Continue 0.8 mile and turn left on Avenue Road. After a half mile, bear left onto Jug End Road and continue 0.3 mile to a turnout on the right where the Appalachian Trail emerges from the woods. Park in the turnout.

GPS Coordinates: 42.1444 N, 73.4316 W

Contact: Jug End State Reservation and Wild-life Management Area, RD East St., Mount Washington, MA 01258, 413/528-0330. Massachusetts Division of State Parks and Recreation, 251 Causeway St., Suite 600, Boston, MA 02114-2104, 617/626-1250, www.mass. gov/dcr/parks/western/juge.htm.

26 MOUNT EVERETT
5.4 mi/3.5 hr   🏃3 ⛰8

in the town of Mount Washington

BEST (

Mount Everett, at 2,602 feet, is among the taller of those little hills in southwestern Massachusetts with the green, rounded tops and steep flanks that seem close enough for

swamp at the base of Mount Everett

someone standing in the valley to reach out and touch. Long views east from atop Everett make it a good place to catch sun rising across the charming landscape of rolling hills and countryside. As a bonus, you pass several waterfalls on the way to Mount Everett's peak. This hike climbs about 1,900 feet.

From the kiosk, follow the Race Brook Trail. Not far up the trail, a sign marks a side path leading right to a view of the lower falls along Race Brook. The main trail bears left and grows steeper just before crossing the brook below upper Race Brook Falls, some 80 feet high—an impressive sight at times of high runoff, most common in the spring. Above the falls, you reach a ledge with a view east. The trail then descends slightly to a third crossing of the brook.

At the Appalachian Trail (AT), marked by signs, turn right (north) for the remaining 0.7 mile to Everett's summit. You are now walking on bare rock exposed by the footsteps of the many hikers who have come before you—thousands of whom were backpacking the entire white-blazed AT from Georgia to Maine. Notice how thin and worn the soil is

on the path, a good lesson in how hiker traffic erodes even the most well-cared for of trails. The views eastward begin before the summit, where only stunted trees and vegetation grow. In this rural southwest corner of Massachusetts, the valley and expanse of wooded hills show amazingly few signs of human presence. An abandoned fire tower (unsafe to climb) marks the summit; walk close to it for views toward the Catskills. Hike down along the same route.

User Groups: Hikers and leashed dogs. This trail is not suitable for bikes or horses; no wheelchair facilities.

Permits: Parking and access are free.

Maps: A free trail map of Mount Washington State Forest, which covers Mount Everett, is available at the state forest headquarters or at the Massachusetts Division of State Parks and Recreation website. A map of area trails is available from the Appalachian Mountain Club (Northern Berkshires/Southwestern Massachusetts/Wachusett Mountain, $5.95). For a topographic area map, request Ashley Falls from the USGS.

Directions: From the junction where Routes

23 and 41 split in Egremont, follow Route 41 south for 5.2 miles to a turnout on the right. A kiosk and blue blazes mark the start of the Race Brook Trail.

GPS Coordinates: 42.0861 N, 73.4144 W

Contact: Mount Washington State Forest, RD 3 East St., Mount Washington, MA 01258, 413/528-0330. Massachusetts Division of State Parks and Recreation, 251 Causeway St., Suite 600, Boston, MA 02114-2104, 617/626-1250, www.mass.gov/dcr/parks/western/meve.htm.

27 THE RIGA PLATEAU
17 mi/2 days

between Egremont, Massachusetts, and Salisbury, Connecticut

BEST (

This very popular Appalachian Trail stretch offers easy hiking along a low ridge with numerous long views of the green hills and rural countryside that so beautifully mark this quiet corner of New England. Expect to see lots of day hikers and backpackers on warm weekends here, with shelters and camping areas tending to fill to overflowing; midweek, however, the campsite and trail are sparsely populated. Or try coming here in May, after the trails and woods have dried out, but before the summer crowds, high temperatures, and swarms of mosquitoes arrive. The cumulative elevation gained over the course of this hike is about 3,500 feet.

From the turnout on Jug End Road, follow the white blazes of the Appalachian Trail (AT) southbound. The trail ascends gently, then steeply, through the woods to Jug End at 1.1 miles, the northern tip of the so-called Riga Plateau, with wide views northward to the Berkshire Mountains. On a clear day, Mount Greylock, the highest peak in Massachusetts, is visible in the distance. Now you're on the ridge, with only fairly easy climbs and dips ahead. The trail passes several open ledges on the Mount Bushnell ascent, reaching its 1,834-foot summit at 2.3 miles. Easy woods walking leads you into the Mount Everett State Reservation, crossing a road at 3.9 miles; a short distance to the right is serene Guilder Pond, a worthwhile detour. Continuing on the AT, the trail steepens a bit to a fire tower at 4.3 miles and Everett's summit (2,602 ft.) at 4.6 miles, with breathtaking views in all directions.

The AT descends off Everett at an easy slope and heads back into the woods, then climbs slightly to the open, rocky Race Mountain crown, 6.4 miles into this hike and 2,365 feet above the ocean. The trail follows the crest of cliffs with wide views northeast to southeast of the Housatonic Valley. At 8.1 miles, you pass near Bear Rock Falls (on the left) and its namesake camping area. Beyond here, the trail descends steadily, then a bit more steeply into the dark defile of Sages Ravine, another camping area at 9.6 miles, as the AT enters Connecticut.

The AT follows the ravine, then leaves it for the most strenuous part of this hike, the 1.4-mile climb to the 2,316-foot Bear Mountain summit, the highest peak in Connecticut. From the top of Bear, at 10.9 miles, the trail descends steadily, if easily, over open terrain with long views of Connecticut's northwestern corner before reentering the woods. The Undermountain Trail turns sharply left at 11.8 miles; continue straight ahead on the AT, soon passing the Brassie Brook, Ball Brook, and Riga camping areas. The forest along here is bright and, although trees block the views, you're on the ridge and it feels high.

Stay southbound on the AT, soon climbing more steeply to reach the open ledges of the Lion's Head at 14.2 miles, with some of the hike's best views of a bucolic countryside, including the town of Salisbury, CT, and Prospect Mountain straight ahead. Double back a short distance from the Lion's Head ledges and descend on the AT, passing a junction with the Lion's Head Trail. The trail now descends at a steady grade through quiet woods, reaching the parking lot on Route 41 at 17 miles from Jug End Road.

Camping is permitted only at designated

shelters and campsites along this section of the Appalachian Trail. From north to south, they are: Glen Brook shelter, reached via a short side trail off the AT, 3.4 miles into this hike; a campsite 0.4 mile off the AT down the Race Brook Falls Trail, 5.3 miles into this hike; the Bear Rock Falls campsite, beside the AT at 8.1 miles; Sages Ravine at 9.6 miles; the Brassie Brook shelter and campsites at 12.3 miles; the Ball Brook campsite at 12.9 miles; the Riga camping area at 13.5 miles; and the Plateau campsite at 13.7 miles, a short distance from the hike's end. Campfires are prohibited from Bear Rock Falls campsite south to the Plateau campsite. Campers must cook with portable camp stoves.

User Groups: Hikers and dogs. Bikes and horses are prohibited; no wheelchair facilities.

Permits: Parking and access are free.

Maps: See maps 3 and 4 in the Map and Guide to the Appalachian Trail in Massachusetts and Connecticut, a five-map set and guidebook available for $19.95 ($14.95 for the maps alone) from the Appalachian Trail Conservancy. For topographic area maps, request Great Barrington, Ashley Falls, and Sharon from the USGS.

Directions: You need to shuttle two vehicles to make this one-way traverse. To hike north to south, as described here, leave one vehicle in the Appalachian Trail parking lot on Route 41 in Salisbury, CT, 0.8 mile north of the junction of Routes 44 and 41. To reach this hike's start, drive your second vehicle north on Route 41 to Egremont. Just before reaching Route 23, turn left onto Mount Washington Road. Continue 0.8 mile and turn left on Avenue Road. At a half mile, bear to the left onto Jug End Road and continue 0.3 mile to a turnout on the right where the Appalachian Trail emerges from the woods. Park in the turnout.

GPS Coordinates: 42.1445 N, 73.4314 W

Contact: Appalachian Trail Conservancy, 799 Washington St., P.O. Box 807, Harpers Ferry, WV 25425-0807, 304/535-6331, www.appalachiantrail.org.

28 BASH BISH FALLS

0.5 mi/0.75 hr   👫2 ⚠10

in Bash Bish Falls State Park in Mount Washington

BEST (

After driving along what has to be one of the most winding roads in Massachusetts, you hike this extremely short trail to what may be the state's most spectacular waterfall. As the Bash Bish Brook tumbles through a vertical stack of giant boulders, it splits into twin columns of water on either side of a huge, triangular block; then settles briefly in a clear, deep pool at the base of the falls before dropping in a foaming torrent through the water-carved rock walls of Bash Bish Gorge. The falls are, predictably, enhanced by spring rains and snowmelt and are much thinner in fall. The Bash Bish Falls Trail is well marked with blue triangles and only a quarter-mile walk downhill from the roadside turnout leads to the falls.

User Groups: Hikers and leashed dogs. This trail is not suitable for bikes or horses; no wheelchair facilities.

Permits: Parking and access are free.

Maps: Although no map is needed for this hike, a free area trail map is available at the Mount Washington State Forest headquarters or at the Massachusetts Division of State Parks and Recreation website. This area is covered in the Northern Berkshires/Southwestern Massachusetts/Wachusett Mountain map, $5.95 in paper, available from the Appalachian Mountain Club. For a topographic area map, request Ashley Falls from the USGS.

Directions: From the junction of Routes 23 and 41 in Egremont, drive south on Route 41 for 0.1 mile and turn right onto Mount Washington Road, which becomes East Street. Follow the signs several miles to Bash Bish Falls State Park and a turnout on the left. To reach the Mount Washington State Forest headquarters, follow the signs from East Street.

GPS Coordinates: 42.1152 N, 73.4917 W

Contact: Mount Washington State Forest, RD 3 East St., Mount Washington, MA 01258,

413/528-0330. Massachusetts Division of State Parks and Recreation, 251 Causeway St., Suite 600, Boston, MA 02114-2104, 617/626-1250, www.mass.gov/dcr/parks/western/mwas.htm.

29 ALANDER MOUNTAIN
5.6 mi/3 hr   4 9

in Mount Washington State Forest in Mount Washington

Less than a mile from the New York border and a few miles from Connecticut, Alander Mountain (2,240 ft.) has two broad, flat summits. The westernmost summit has the best views of the southern Berkshires and of the hills and farmland of eastern New York, all the way to the Catskill Mountains. An open ridge running south from the summit offers even more sweeping views. A fun adventure for hikers of all levels, this fairly easy climb nets an elevation gain of 500 feet.

From the kiosk behind the headquarters, the Alander Mountain Trail gradually ascends a woods road for much of its distance, then narrows to a trail and grows steeper. Just past the first-come, first-served state forest cabin site, a sign points left to the east summit loop and right to the west summit loop; both loops take just minutes to walk. The west loop offers great views to the north, east, and south. At the mountain's true summit are three old concrete blocks, probably the foundation of a former fire tower. Continue over the summit on the white-blazed South Taconic Trail for views westward into New York. Turn back and descend the way you came.

Special note: By hiking northbound from Alander's summit on the scenic South Taconic Trail, you can reach Bash Bish Falls (see *Bash Bish Falls* listing in this chapter) and then return to Alander, adding four miles round-trip to this hike's distance.

Backcountry camping is available in the Mount Washington State Forest at 15 wilderness campsites, 1.5 miles from the trailhead, and in a cabin that sleeps six just below Alander's summit. The cabin (which has a wood-burning stove) and the campsites are filled on a first-come, first-served basis.

User Groups: Hikers, bikers, leashed dogs, and horses; no wheelchair facilities. During the winter watch out for snowmobiles on this trail.

Permits: Parking and access are free.

Maps: An area trail map is available from the Appalachian Mountain Club (Northern Berkshires/Southwestern Massachusetts/Wachusett Mountain, $5.95). A free map of Mount Washington State Forest is available at the state forest headquarters or at the Massachusetts Division of State Parks and Recreation website. For a topographic area map, request Ashley Falls from the USGS.

Directions: From the junction of Routes 23 and 41 in Egremont, drive south on Route 41 for 0.1 mile and turn right onto Mount Washington Road, which becomes East Street. Follow the signs about nine miles to the Mount Washington State Forest headquarters on the right. The blue-blazed Alander Mountain Trail begins behind the headquarters.

GPS Coordinates: 42.0842 N, 73.4665 W

Contact: Mount Washington State Forest, RD 3 East St., Mount Washington, MA 01258, 413/528-0330. Massachusetts Division of State Parks and Recreation, 251 Causeway St., Suite 600, Boston, MA 02114-2104, 617/626-1250, www.mass.gov/dcr/parks/western/mwas.htm.

30 GRANVILLE STATE FOREST: HUBBARD RIVER GORGE
6 mi/2.5 hr   2 9

in Granville State Forest in Granville

Located along the southern border of Massachusetts in the towns of Granville and Tolland, Granville State Forest borders with

© HEIDI J. BROWN

Hubbard River Gorge, Granville State Forest

Connecticut's Tunxis State Forest to create a true sense of tranquil remoteness. Formerly the hunting and fishing grounds of the Tunxis tribe, later open farmland and pastures, and now slowly reverting back into a northern hardwood-conifer forest, this out-and-back hike features the highlight of this out-of-the-way state forest: Hubbard River Gorge, a stunning, 2.5-mile long series of cascades and waterfalls.

From the dirt parking lot, backtrack over the bridge and turn right onto a paved road leading a half mile to the now-closed Hubbard River Campground. The Hubbard River Trail begins at the road's end. Follow the trail, an old woods road marked by blue triangles bearing a hiker symbol, southeast along the Hubbard River. After turning briefly away from the river, the road hugs the rim of the spectacular gorge, passing many spots that

afford views of the river and cascades. Follow the trail as far as you like, then turn around and return the same way. If you go all the way to an old woods road marked on the map as Hartland Hollow Road before turning back, the round-trip is six miles. If you'd like to see another area similar to the Hubbard River Gorge, turn left and hike upstream (north) along Hartland Hollow Road. Watch for the stream through the trees to your right; you'll discover a small gorge and pools in there within less than a half mile from the Hubbard River Trail.

Special note: This quiet corner of Massachusetts is a wonderfully charming area to drive through or, better yet, bicycle. The quaint rural villages of Granville and West Granville are both on the National Register of Historic Districts.

User Groups: Hikers, bikers, leashed dogs, and

horses. No wheelchair facilities. Swimming in the Hubbard River is prohibited under penalty of fine.

Permits: Parking and access are free.

Maps: A free map of hiking trails is available at the sate forest headquarters or at the Massachusetts Division of State Parks and Recreation website. For a topographic area map, request Southwick from the USGS.

Directions: From the junction of Routes 189 and 57 in Granville, drive six miles west on Route 57 and turn left onto West Hartland Road. In another 0.6 mile, you pass a sign for the Granville State Forest; the rough dirt road heading left from that point is where this loop hike will emerge. Continue another 0.3 mile, cross the bridge over the Hubbard River, and park in the dirt lot on the left. The state forest headquarters is on West Hartland Road, 0.6 mile beyond the bridge.

GPS Coordinates: 42.0576 N, 72.9635 W

Contact: Granville State Forest, 323 West Hartland Rd., Granville, MA 01034, 413/357-6611. Massachusetts Division of State Parks and Recreation, 251 Causeway St., Suite 600, Boston, MA 02114-2104, 617/626-1250, www.mass.gov/dcr/parks/western/gran.htm.

CENTRAL
MASSACHUSETTS

Massachusetts at its midsection is a rumpled

blanket of rolling hills, thick forest, and a string of low but craggy summits that rise above the trees to give long views of the surrounding landscape. Far enough away from Boston, but without the same tourist crowds as the Berkshire region, trails to the top of such notable peaks as Mount Holyoke, Wachusett Mountain, and Mount Wataic tend to be quiet, uncrowded, and easy to reach. These are hikes that are great for beginners and kids as well as serious hikers and backpackers trying to get their legs in shape for more strenuous trips elsewhere. Beyond these hills, you will mostly find pleasant woods walks that are easy to moderately difficult and a number of shorter treks leading to gorges, caves, and lush mountain meadows.

Central Massachusetts is also home to two long-distance trails, both of which are largely used by day hikers. The white-blazed Metacomet-Monadnock Trail (Crag Mountain, Mount Holyoke) bounces along the Holyoke Range and through the hills of north-central Massachusetts on its 117-mile course from the Massachusetts/Connecticut line near Agawam and Southwick to the summit of Mount Monadnock in Jaffrey, New Hampshire. In 2009, the federal government designated the Metacomet-Monadnock Trail as part of the new New England National Scenic

Trail, a 200-mile trail route comprised of the Metacomet-Monadnock Trail and the Mattabesett Trail in Connecticut. The blue-blazed Midstate Trail extends 92 miles from Douglas (on the Rhode Island border) to the New Hampshire line at Ashburham, crossing through woods and over small hills. Significant stretches of both trails are on private land, so be aware of and respect any closures.

This area is snow country in Massachusetts, with the hilly terrain near Worcester and Leominster usually racking up the highest annual snowfall totals in the state. Trails in mid-Massachusetts usually become free of snow sometime between mid-March and mid-April, though they often will be muddy for a few weeks after the snow melts (New England's infamous mud season).

Many of the hikes in this chapter are in state parks and forests, where dogs must be leashed; horses are allowed in most state forests and parks, as is hunting in season. Trails leading to the Quabbin Reservoir, one of the largest artificially-made public water supplies in the United States, have special access rules: dogs are prohibited and hikers and mountain bikers should be aware that trails may be closed or rerouted and public access suspended at any time in order to maintain water supply safety.

CENTRAL MASSACHUSETTS

NEW HAMPSHIRE

RHODE ISLAND

CONNECTICUT

see Boston and Cape Cod page 80

see The Berkshires page 26

© AVALON TRAVEL

5 mi
5 km

Littleton
Groton
Harvard
Townsend
Leominster
Fitchburg
Ashburnham
Winchendon
Baldwinville
Gardner
Athol
Royalston
Warwick
Northfield
Millers Falls
Wendell
New Salem
Shutesbury
Amherst
Pelham
Petersham
Barre
Gilbertville
Princeton
Paxton
Worcester
Spencer
West Brookfield
Ware
Belchertown
Ludlow
Hadley
Northampton
Shelburne Falls
Ashfield
Goshen
Westfield
West Springfield
Springfield
Holyoke
Granby
Monson
Palmer
Brimfield
Wales
Sturbridge
Southbridge
West Sutton
Douglas
Uxbridge
Northbridge
Grafton
Northborough
West Boylston
Sterling
Clinton
Marlborough
Unionville

Quabbin Reservoir

1 2 3 4 5 6-8 9-12 13 14 15 16 17 18 19 20-21

1 NORTHFIELD MOUNTAIN: ROSE LEDGE

4.2 mi/2.5 hr   🏃3 ⛰8

in Northfield

The Northfield Mountain Recreation and Environmental Center's 25 miles of hiking and multi-use trails comprise one of the best trail systems open year-round in Massachusetts. The Metacomet-Monadnock Trail is not far from this system and can be reached via a marked trail off the 10th Mountain Trail, near Bugaboo Pass on Northfield Mountain. Other activities, including orienteering, canoeing on the nearby Connecticut River, and educational programs, are conducted through the center. This hike takes in some of the mountain's best features—including the Rose Ledge cliffs and a view of the reservoir at the 1,100-foot summit—but many other loop options are possible here. The route described here climbs about 600–700 feet in elevation.

From the parking lot and visitors center, follow the wide carriage road of the 10th Mountain Trail to the right. Reaching a trail sign 0.1 mile from the parking lot, turn left onto the Rose Ledge Trail footpath, marked here by blue diamonds. Follow the trail 0.2 mile across a carriage road and then turn right with the trail (note the trail is now orange-blazed). In the next 0.8 mile, the trail crosses two carriage roads, Hemlock Hill and Jug End, and then bears left at the fork to traverse above the cliffs, with some views of nearby wooded hills. Just before reaching the wide carriage road called Rock Oak Ramble, turn right at an easily overlooked connector trail leading downhill a short distance to the Lower Ledge Trail. Turn left on the Lower Ledge and you're soon walking below the cliffs and may see rock climbers on them; be careful of loose rock falling from above if you venture near the cliff base. At 1.4 miles, the Lower Ledge Trail rejoins the Rose Ledge Trail. Continuing on as a steady uphill climb through the woods, in another 0.6 mile, the Summit Trail enters on the left and coincides with the Rose Ledge Trail for the final 0.2 mile uphill push to the summit. From the viewing platform, enjoy the watery vista of Northfield Reservoir. On the return trip, follow the Reservoir Road off the summit, staying on the road for about 0.1 mile until reaching a junction with the Bobcat Trail. Turn left on the trail and follow downhill a little less than two miles back to the parking area, passing the Chocolate Pot shelter a little more than halfway down.

User Groups: Hikers and leashed dogs. No bikes, horses, or wheelchair facilities. Bikes and horses are allowed on multi-use trails (not included in this hike), but bikers must register once per season at the visitors center and horseback riders must check in for parking and trail information; helmets are required for both biking and horseback riding. Trails are often closed to bikes and horses during mud season, usually until late April.

Permits: Northfield Mountain is a pumped storage hydroelectric facility owned and operated by FirstLight Power Resources. No fee is charged for parking or trail use.

Maps: A trail map is available at the visitors center and online from Northfield Mountain Recreation and Environmental Center. For topographic area maps, request Northfield and Orange from the USGS.

Directions: From the junction of the Routes 63 and 10 in Northfield, drive south on Route 63 to a left turn for the Northfield Mountain visitors center and recreation parking area. The visitors center is open 9 A.M.–5 P.M. Wednesday–Sunday, spring–fall. The cross-country center is open 9 A.M.–5 P.M. daily during the ski season.

GPS Coordinates: 42.6110 N, 72.4720 W

Contact: Northfield Mountain Recreation and Environmental Center, 99 Millers Falls Rd./Rte. 63, Northfield, MA 01360, 413/659-3714, www.firstlightpower.com/northfield.

② CRAG MOUNTAIN
3.4 mi/2 hr

in Northfield

One of the rocky outcroppings of Northfield's Bald Hills region, this easy hike—ascending only a few hundred feet—leads to Crag Mountain (1,503 ft.) and expansive views from its open, knife-edge summit. From the mountain's center-of-New England locale, take in the Berkshires and the southern Green Mountains of Vermont to the west and northwest, New Hampshire's Mount Monadnock to the northeast, the central hills of Massachusetts to the east, and the nearby Northfield Mountain Reservoir, Mount Toby, and South Sugarloaf Mountain to the south.

From the parking turnout, follow the white blazes of the Metacomet-Monadnock Trail as it heads south into the woods. Not far from the trailhead, the path crosses one wet area and then begins its gentle rise through a mixed deciduous and conifer forest. Breaking out of the woods and crossing on rockier terrain just yards from the top, the trail reaches Crag's open summit ridge 1.7 miles from the road. Enjoy the scenery and hike back along the same route.

User Groups: Hikers and dogs. No bikes, horses, or wheelchair facilities.

Permits: Parking and access are free.

Maps: A map of this trail is included with The Metacomet-Monadnock Trail Guide, available for $14.95 from the AMC Berkshire Chapter. For a topographic area map, request Northfield from the USGS.

Directions: From Route 10/63 in Northfield, about 0.2 mile south of the town center and 0.3 mile north of the southern junction of Routes 10 and 63, turn west onto Maple Street, which becomes Gulf Road. Drive 3.1 miles to a turnout on the right, where the white blazes of the Metacomet-Monadnock Trail enter the woods.

GPS Coordinates: 42.6603 N, 72.4182 W

Contact: AMC Berkshire Chapter, P.O. Box 9369, North Amherst, MA 01059. (The

Appalachian Mountain Club's Berkshire's chapter is charged with maintaining portions of the Metacomet-Monadnock Trail crossing private land.)

③ BEAR'S DEN
0.2 mi/0.5 hr

in New Salem

This compact but dramatic gorge along the Middle Branch of the Swift River is a beautiful spot hidden away just steps from the road. From the parking area, follow the left fork of the trail to reach the gorge rim, which, in just a few feet, places you at the brink of a precipitous drop to the river. Double back and follow the trail downhill to the banks of the river, where the foundations of an old grist mill still stand. A sign near the trail's beginning relates some of this spot's history: how a settler killed a black bear here, thus explaining the name Bear's Den, and how the Wampanoag chief King Phillip supposedly met with other chiefs here in 1675 during their wars with European settlers in the Connecticut Valley.

User Groups: Hikers and dogs. No wheelchair facilities. This trail is not suitable for bikes, horses, or skis.

Permits: Parking and access are free.

Maps: No map is necessary for this short and easy walk.

Directions: From the junction of Routes 202 and 122 in New Salem, follow Route 202 south for 0.4 mile. Turn right onto Elm Street, drive 0.7 mile, and then turn left onto Neilson Road. Drive a half mile and park at the roadside. The entrance is on the right, where a short trail leads to the gorge. The reservation is open to the public sunrise–sunset year-round.

GPS Coordinates: 42.5438 N, 72.3206 W

Contact: The Trustees of Reservations Central Region Office, Doyle Reservation, 325 Lindell Ave., Leominster, MA 01453-5414, 978/840-4446, www.thetrustees.org.

4 MOUNT WATATIC AND NUTTING HILL
2.8 mi/1.5 hr

in Ashburnham

The scenic southern terminus of the long-distance Wapack footpath, 1,832-foot Mount Watatic's pair of barren, rocky summit ledges offer excellent views of nearby peaks such as Wachusett Mountain and Kidder and Temples Mountains. The views extend north into North Hampshire and, on a clear day, to landmarks as distant as Mount Greylock, the White Mountains, and even the Boston skyline. The Midstate Trail was rerouted in recent years to coincide with the Wapack Trail over Watatic's summit; both are well blazed with yellow triangles. This hike leads first to Watatic's scenic outcropping, Nutting Hill.

From the parking area, follow an old woods road north, ascending gradually. At 0.3 mile, the Wapack/Midstate Trail turns right (east), but this hike continues straight ahead on the blue-blazed State Line Trail to reach Nutting Hill. A half mile farther, you reach a junction where the State Line Trail forks left; continue straight ahead on the Midstate Trail (yellow-blazed), which is rejoined by the Wapack Trail within another 0.2 mile. It is nearly a mile to Watatic's summit from this point. Soon passing over Nutting Hill's open top and veering to the right, watch for the cairns marking the way. Reentering the woods, you climb Watatic's northwest slope, passing by the somewhat overgrown trails of the former Mount Watatic ski area. Just below the summit stands an abandoned fire tower, now closed and unsafe. From the summit, an unmarked path leads to the lower, southeast summit. Double back to the fire tower, turn left, and follow the Wapack, passing an open ledge with views and, farther down, an enormous split boulder. At the Midstate Trail junction, turn left for the parking area.

User Groups: Hikers and dogs. This trail is not suitable for bikes or horses; no wheelchair facilities.

Permits: Parking and access are free.

Maps: A map and guide to the Wapack Trail, including this hike, is available for $11 from the Friends of the Wapack. For a topographic area map, request Ashburnham from the USGS.

Directions: The trailhead parking area is on the north side of Route 119 in Ashburnham, 1.4 miles west of its junction with Route 101.

GPS Coordinates: 42.6870 N, 71.8901 W

Contact: Friends of the Wapack, P.O. Box 115, West Peterborough, NH 03468, www.wapack.org.

5 WILLARD BROOK
2 mi/1 hr

in Willard Brook State Forest in Ashby

A good, gentle hike for introducing very young children to the woods, this easy walk hugs the rock-strewn Willard Brook through its tight valley, winding through hemlock groves and among huge boulders. The trail begins from either side of the stone bridge over Willard Brook, just below Damon Pond. Toward the other (northeast) end of the trail, it ascends a hillside and reaches a forest road; turning left brings you shortly to the state forest headquarters. Most people just double back to the start for a nice two-mile stroll. There are several miles of woods roads in the state forest open to other activities, such as mountain biking or horseback riding.

User Groups: Hikers and leashed dogs. No bikes, horses, or wheelchair facilities.

Permits: A daily parking fee of $5 is collected mid-May–mid-October.

Maps: A free, basic trail map of the state forest is available at the headquarters on Route 119 in West Townsend, just before the Ashby town line, or at the Massachusetts Division of State Parks and Recreation website. For a

covered bridge crossing of Willard Brook, Ashby

topographic area map, request Ashburnham from the USGS.

Directions: From the junction of Routes 119 and 31 in Ashby, drive 0.2 mile east on Route 119 to the Damon Pond entrance and parking area.

GPS Coordinates: 42.6870 N, 71.8901 W

Contact: Willard Brook State Forest, Rte. 119, West Townsend, MA 01474, 978/597-8802. Massachusetts Division of State Parks and Recreation, 251 Causeway St., Suite 600, Boston, MA 02114-2104, 617/626-1250, www.state.ma.us/dem/forparks.htm.

6 CROW HILLS

0.7 mi/0.75 hr   2 △ 9

in Leominster State Forest in Westminster

The hike up Crow Hills, at the western edge of the more than 4,000-acre Leominster State Forest, is a short loop that can be done with young children, though the trail does grow steep and rocky in a few small sections. Despite its brevity and the climb of just a few hundred feet, it is one of the most dramatic walks in central Massachusetts, traversing the top of tall cliffs with commanding views of the wooded hills and ponds of the state forest and nearby Wachusett Mountain. Climb the hills in early autumn and the vivid crimson-colored woods may convince you to make this trek an annual event.

From the parking lot, cross Route 31 to a wide, well-marked trail entering the woods. Within 100 feet, the trail turns sharply left, then swings right and climbs steeply to the base of cliffs, 100 feet high in places. The trail then diverges right and left, with both branches looping up to the cliff tops. You can hike the loop in either direction; this description leads to the right (counterclockwise). Walk below the cliff to where stones arranged in steps lead steeply uphill to a junction with the Midstate Trail, marked by yellow triangular blazes. Turn left, carefully following the trail atop the cliffs past several spots that offer sweeping views; the best views are at the far end of the cliffs. Wachusett Mountain, with its ski slopes, is visible to the southwest. Take care not to kick any loose stones or wander near the cliff's edge as there are often rock climbers and hikers below. From the last open ledges, the Midstate Trail swings right, entering the woods again and continuing about 75 yards, then turning left and descending a steep, rocky gully. At its bottom, turn left again and, diverging from the Midstate, walk the trail around the base of the cliffs to this loop's beginning. Turn right and descend to the parking lot.

User Groups: Hikers and leashed dogs. This trail is not suitable for bikes or horses; no wheelchair facilities.

Permits: A $5 parking fee is collected May–October; a season pass costs $35. The parking lot may not always be plowed in winter; call the state forest headquarters for more information.

Maps: A free, basic trail map of Leominster State Forest is available at the state forest headquarters or at the Massachusetts Division of State Parks and Recreation website. The Mount Wachusett and Leominster State Forest Trail Map costs $3.95 from New England Cartographics (413/549-4124 or toll-free 888/995-6277, www.necartographics.com). For a topographic area map, request Fitchburg from the USGS.

Directions: The hike begins from a large parking lot at the Crow Hills Pond Picnic Area along Route 31 on the Westminster/Princeton line, 2.2 miles south of the junction of Routes 31 and 2 and 1.5 miles north of the junction of Routes 31 and 140.

GPS Coordinates: 42.5351 N, 71.8541 W

Contact: Leominster State Forest, Rte. 31, Princeton, MA 01541, 978/874-2303. Massachusetts Division of State Parks and Recreation, 251 Causeway St., Suite 600, Boston, MA 02114-2104, 617/626-1250, www.state.ma.us/dem/forparks.htm.

⑦ BALL HILL LOOP

3.5 mi/2.5 hr

in Leominster State Forest in Westminster, Princeton, and Leominster

Leominster State Forest has a network of marked trails and less-distinct footpaths weaving throughout, most in its northern half, north of Rocky Pond Road/Parmenter Road. (South of that dirt road, which is open to bikes but not motor vehicles, the state forest is crossed mainly by old woods roads.) This hike ascends one of the low, wooded hills in the state forest into an area where even frequent visitors to Leominster find it easy to stumble across trails they don't recognize. There are myriad trails through here and it's easy to get lost once you venture over Ball Hill. Nonetheless, the woodlands are quiet and fun to explore. This hike ascends small hills but never climbs more than a few hundred feet.

From the parking area, walk across the earthen dike between the two halves of Crow Hills Pond and then turn right, following a blazed trail south along the shore of the pond. Within a half mile, turn left (east) onto the Rocky Pond Trail, which climbs Ball Hill, steeply for short stretches. Near the hilltop, about one mile from the hike's start, is a spot where the trees thin enough to allow a partially obstructed view of the hills to the west. Anyone concerned about getting lost might want to turn back from here. Otherwise, continue over the hill, through quiet woods crossed by the occasional stone wall.

Descending the back side of the hill, ignore the trails branching off to the right. Turn left at the first opportunity: about 2.5 miles from the parking area, where you see a landfill through the trees at the state forest edge. The trail swings north, then west; continue bearing left at trail junctions. On your way back, you pass through a wet area, over a low hillock, and eventually reach the paved parking lot at the public beach at the Crow Hills Pond's north end. Cross the parking lot to the south (left),

a Medusa-like tree growing in Leominster State Forest

picking up the trail again for the short walk back to the dike across the pond.

User Groups: Hikers and leashed dogs. This trail is not suitable for bikes or horses; no wheelchair facilities.

Permits: A $5 parking fee is collected May–October; a season pass costs $35. The parking lot may not always be plowed in winter; call the state forest headquarters for more information.

Maps: A free, basic trail map of Leominster State Forest is available at the state forest headquarters or at the Massachusetts Division of State Parks and Recreation website. The Mount Wachusett and Leominster State Forest Trail Map costs $3.95 from New England Cartographics (413/549-4124 or toll-free 888/995-6277, www.necartographics.com). For a topographic area map, request Fitchburg from the USGS.

Directions: The hike begins from a large parking lot at the Crow Hills Pond Picnic Area along Route 31 on the Westminster-Princeton line, 2.2 miles south of the junction of Routes 31 and 2 and 1.5 miles north of the junction of Routes 31 and 140.

GPS Coordinates: 42.5351 N, 71.8541 W

Contact: Leominster State Forest, Rte. 31, Princeton, MA 01541, 978/874-2303. Massachusetts Division of State Parks and Recreation, 251 Causeway St., Suite 600, Boston, MA 02114-2104, 617/626-1250, www.state.ma.us/dem/forparks.htm.

8 LEOMINSTER FOREST ROADS LOOP

5.5 mi/2.5 hr   🥾3 ⛰7

in Leominster State Forest in Westminster, Princeton, and Leominster

This loop of approximately 5.5 miles largely follows old forest roads through the southern half of Leominster State Forest, making it particularly fun on a mountain bike or cross-country skis—Leominster is in the Bay State's "snow belt" and regularly sees several feet of snow cover each winter. There are small hills along these roads—nothing that is difficult to hike, but which can make skiing or mountain biking moderately difficult.

From the parking lot, cross the picnic area and the earthen dike dividing the two halves of Crow Hills Pond. Across the dike, turn right (south), following the trail along the pond and past it about 0.7 mile to the dirt Rocky Pond Road (which is not open to motor vehicles). Cross Rocky Pond Road onto Wolf Rock Road and continue about a half mile. Where the road forks, bear right and then watch for an unmarked footpath diverging left within 0.2 mile (if you reach the state forest boundary near private homes, you've gone too far). Follow that winding, narrow path through the woods less than a half mile to Wolf Rock Road and turn right. You descend a steep hill on the road, turn left onto Center Road, and follow it about 1.2 miles to Parmenter Road. Turn left (west), climbing a hill and crossing from Leominster into Princeton, where the road becomes Rocky Pond Road. From the road's high point, continue west for less than a mile to the junction of Rocky Pond Road, Wolf Rock Road, and the trail from Crow Hills Pond; turn right on the trail to return to this hike's start.

Special note: Short sections of this loop follow hiking trails that would be difficult on a bike. Cyclists might instead begin this loop from the dirt parking area and gate where Rocky Pond Road crosses Route 31, 0.6 mile south of the main parking area. Pedal east on Rocky Pond Road for about 0.4 mile and then turn right onto the wide Wolf Rock Road. A half mile farther, where the road forks, bear left, staying on Wolf Rock Road, which leads to Center Road and the continuation of this hike.

User Groups: Hikers, bikers, and leashed dogs. No horses or wheelchair facilities.

Permits: A $5 parking fee is collected May–October; a season pass costs $35. The parking lot may not always be plowed in winter; call the state forest headquarters for more information.

Maps: A free, basic trail map of Leominster State Forest is available at the state forest headquarters or at the Massachusetts Division

fallen autumn leaves, Leominster State Forest

of State Parks and Recreation website. The Mount Wachusett and Leominster State Forest Trail Map costs $3.95 from New England Cartographics (413/549-4124 or toll-free 888/995-6277, www.necartographics.com). For a topographic area map, request Fitchburg from the USGS.

Directions: The hike begins from a large parking lot at the Crow Hills Pond Picnic Area along Route 31 on the Westminster/Princeton line, 2.2 miles south of the junction of Routes 31 and 2 and 1.5 miles north of the junction of Routes 31 and 140.

GPS Coordinates: 42.5351 N, 71.8541 W

Contact: Leominster State Forest, Rte. 31, Princeton, MA 01541, 978/874-2303. Massachusetts Division of State Parks and Recreation, 251 Causeway St., Suite 600, Boston, MA 02114-2104, 617/626-1250, www.state.ma.us/dem/forparks.htm.

9 WACHUSETT MOUNTAIN: BALANCED ROCK

0.6 mi/0.5 hr   𝄜2 △7

in Wachusett Mountain State Reservation in Princeton

Balanced Rock is a glacial-erratic boulder that well lives up to its name. Pick up the Midstate Trail's yellow triangular blazes from the parking lot, behind and to the right of the lodge. Here the trail is also known as the Balanced Rock Trail. Follow it, climbing gently, for 0.3 mile to Balanced Rock. To finish this hike, return the way you came. Hikers looking for a bit more of an outing can continue on the Midstate Trail to the Wachusett summit via the Semuhenna and Harrington Trails and then descend the Old Indian Trail back to the Midstate Trail to return for a loop of several miles. Consult the map and inquire at the visitors center for specific distances.

User Groups: Hikers and leashed dogs. Bikes and horses are prohibited; no wheelchair facilities.

Permits: A daily parking fee of $2 is collected mid-May–mid-October.

Maps: A free contour map of hiking trails is available at the visitors center or at the Massachusetts Division of State Parks and Recreation website. The Mount Wachusett and Leominster State Forest Trail Map costs $3.95 from New England Cartographics (413/549-4124 or toll-free 888/995-6277, www.necartographics.com). For topographic area maps, request Sterling and Fitchburg from the USGS.

Directions: From Route 140, 2.2 miles south of the junction of Routes 140 and 2 in Westminster and 1.8 miles north of the junction of Routes 140 and 31, turn onto Mile Hill Road, following signs to the Wachusett Mountain Ski Area. Drive a mile, turn right into the ski area parking lot, and then cross to the rear of the lot, behind the lodge. The Wachusett Mountain State Reservation Visitor Center is farther up Mile Hill Road.

GPS Coordinates: 42.5114 N, 71.8866 W

Contact: Wachusett Mountain State Reservation, Mountain Rd., P.O. Box 248, Princeton, MA 01541, 978/464-2987. Massachusetts Division of State Parks and Recreation, 251 Causeway St., Suite 600, Boston, MA 02114-2104, 617/626-1250, www.state.ma.us/dem/forparks.htm.

10 WACHUSETT MOUNTAIN: PINE HILL TRAIL

2 mi/1.5 hr   𝄜4 △8

in Wachusett Mountain State Reservation in Princeton

At 2,006 feet and the biggest hill in central Massachusetts, Wachusett may be better known for its downhill ski area. But the state reservation has a fairly extensive network of fine hiking trails, including a section of the Midstate Trail that passes over the summit. The summit offers views in all directions: on a clear day, you can see New Hampshire's Mount Monadnock to the north and the Boston skyline 40 miles to the east. Trail junctions are marked with signs. The Pine Hill Trail is a steep, rocky climb that could be dangerous in snowy or icy conditions.

From the visitors center parking lot, follow the Bicentennial Trail about 0.1 mile to the first trail branching off to the right, the Pine Hill Trail—actually an old ski trail and the most direct route to the summit, about a half mile. The trail ascends at a moderate grade over fairly rocky terrain. After checking out the views from various spots on the broad summit, cross to its southwest corner and look for the Harrington Trail sign. Descending the Harrington, you soon cross the paved summit road; after reentering the woods, take a short side path left off the Harrington to enjoy a long view west over the sparsely populated hills and valleys of central Massachusetts. Backtrack and descend the Harrington to the Link Trail, turning left. Turn right onto the Mountain House Trail, descend briefly, and then bear left onto the Loop Trail, which descends to the Bicentennial Trail. Turn left for the visitors center.

User Groups: Hikers and leashed dogs. Bikes and horses are prohibited; no wheelchair facilities.

Permits: A daily parking fee of $2 is collected mid-May–mid-October.

Maps: A free contour map of hiking trails is available at the visitors center at the Massachusetts Division of State Parks and Recreation website. The Mount Wachusett and Leominster State Forest Trail Map costs $3.95 from New England Cartographics (413/549-4124 or toll-free 888/995-6277, www.necartographics.com). For topographic area maps, request Sterling and Fitchburg from the USGS.

Directions: From Route 140, 2.2 miles south of the junction of Routes 140 and 2 in Westminster and 1.8 miles north of the junction of Routes 140 and 31, turn onto Mile Hill Road, following signs to the Wachusett Mountain State Reservation Visitor Center. GPS Coordinates: 42.5114 N, 71.8866 W

Contact: Wachusett Mountain State Reservation, Mountain Rd., P.O. Box 248, Princeton, MA 01541, 978/464-2987. Massachusetts Division of State Parks and Recreation, 251 Causeway St., Suite 600, Boston, MA 02114-2104, 617/626-1250, www.state.ma.us/dem/forparks.htm.

🔟 WACHUSETT MOUNTAIN LOOP
5 mi/3 hr

in Wachusett Mountain State Reservation in Princeton

This hike to the summit of Wachusett (2,006 ft.) follows a circuitous, but enjoyable route up the largest mountain in central Massachusetts, taking advantage of the extensive trail network here. Although sections of the trail are somewhat rocky and steep for brief stretches, it's not very difficult, ascending about 700

feet in elevation. You can easily shorten or lengthen this hike as well; check out the trail map and improvise from this description. A scenic alternative is the Jack Frost Trail, which passes through dense hemlock forest.

From the visitors center parking lot, follow the Bicentennial Trail for about a mile as it contours around the mountain's base, passing three trail junctions, then bear left onto the High Meadow Trail. Follow it across an open meadow and then back into the woods again before reaching Echo Lake. Stay to the left on the gravel road beside the lake for about 0.1 mile, turn left on the Echo Lake Trail, and follow it less than a half mile to a parking lot. Crossing the small lot, pick up the Stage Coach Trail, climbing steadily up an old carriage road, which narrows to a footpath. After more than a half mile, bear right on the Harrington Trail. It crosses West Road, then the Administration Road, before suddenly growing much steeper as it makes a direct line for the summit. But right before that steep part begins, turn left on the Semuhenna Trail, staying on it for about a half mile. Cross the paved summit road, reenter the woods, and then immediately turn right on the West Side Trail. You're on that path for less than a half mile before turning right again on the Old Indian Trail, the steepest part of this hike. As you climb to the summit, you'll pass a ski area chairlift station right before reaching the top. Cross the summit to the paved road that heads down, follow it about 100 feet, and then bear right into the woods on the Mountain House Trail. Descend about a quarter mile, turn left, continue another quarter mile or less, and turn left again on the Loop Trail, descending over rocks to the Bicentennial Trail. Turn left for the visitors center.

User Groups: Hikers and leashed dogs. No bikes, horses, or wheelchair facilities.

Permits: A daily parking fee of $2 is collected mid-May–mid-October.

Maps: A free contour map of hiking trails is available at the visitors center or at the

Massachusetts Division of State Parks and Recreation website. The Mount Wachusett and Leominster State Forest Trail Map costs $3.95 from New England Cartographics (413/549-4124 or toll-free 888/995-6277, www.necartographics.com). For topographic area maps, request Sterling and Fitchburg from the USGS.

Directions: From Route 140, 2.2 miles south of the junction of Routes 140 and 2 in Westminster and 1.8 miles north of the junction of Routes 140 and 31, turn onto Mile Hill Road, following signs to the Wachusett Mountain State Reservation Visitor Center.

GPS Coordinates: 42.5114 N, 71.8866 W

Contact: Wachusett Mountain State Reservation, Mountain Rd., P.O. Box 248, Princeton, MA 01541, 978/464-2987. Massachusetts Division of State Parks and Recreation, 251 Causeway St., Suite 600, Boston, MA 02114-2104, 617/626-1250, www.state.ma.us/dem/forparks.htm.

12 REDEMPTION ROCK TO WACHUSETT MOUNTAIN
1.8 mi/1 hr 🏃2 ⛰7

in Princeton

Legend has it that a Concord settler named John Hoar sat atop this massive, flat-topped boulder with members of a band of Wampanoags in 1676 to negotiate the release of Mary Rowlandson, wife of the minister in the nearby town of Lancaster, whom the Wampanoags had abducted and held captive for 11 weeks. A fun spot to explore with kids, Redemption Rock is just off the roadside. This hike continues past the rock through the woods for a short distance to the base of Wachusett Mountain and back, following a fairly quiet Midstate Trail stretch where you might see a deer or grouse.

After exploring Redemption Rock, which sits beside the parking area, follow the Midstate Trail's yellow triangular blazes into the

woods. Watch closely for the blazes; several side trails branch off the Midstate Trail. It proceeds generally westward through the woods, climbing slightly and traversing some rocky trail stretches and some wet areas, reaching Mountain Road and the parking lot for the Wachusett Mountain Ski Area in 0.9 mile. Turn around and return the way you came or combine this with the Wachusett Mountain: Balanced Rock hike, which begins across the ski area parking lot.

User Groups: Hikers and dogs. The trail is not suitable for bikes or horses; no wheelchair facilities.

Permits: Parking and access are free.

Maps: The Mount Wachusett and Leominster State Forest Trail Map costs $3.95 from New England Cartographics (413/549-4124 or toll-free 888/995-6277, www.necartographics.com). For topographic area maps, request Fitchburg and Sterling from the USGS.

Directions: The hike begins from the small parking lot at Redemption Rock along Route 140 in Princeton, 3.1 miles south of the junction of Routes 140 and 2 in Westminster and 0.9 mile north of the junction of Routes 140 and 31 in Princeton. Redemption Rock is open to the public sunrise–sunset year-round.

GPS Coordinates: 42.4817 N, 71.8475 W

Contact: The Trustees of Reservations Central Region Office, Doyle Reservation, 325 Lindell Ave., Leominster, MA 01453-5414, 978/840-4446, www.thetrustees.org.

13 WACHUSETT MEADOW TO WACHUSETT MOUNTAIN
6.2 mi/3.5 hr 🏃5 ⛰8

in Princeton in the Wachusett Meadow Wildlife Sanctuary

Beginning from Wachusett Meadow, the picturesque 977-acre Audubon wildlife refuge, much of this Midstate Trail stretch is relatively easy, ascending less than 1,000 feet in elevation, much of that over the steep final 0.3-mile climb to the Wachusett Mountain summit, where there are long views in every direction. Visitors to Wachusett Meadow shouldn't miss the 300-year-old Crocker maple, one of the largest sugar maples in the country, with a trunk circumference of more than 15 feet. It sits on the west edge of the meadow, a very short detour off this hike's route, and it is guaranteed to awe children and adults alike.

From the wildlife sanctuary parking area, walk north into the meadow on the Mountain Trail and then turn left in the middle of the meadow at post six, heading for the woods and reaching a junction with the Midstate Trail about 0.2 mile from the parking lot. Turn right (north), following the Midstate over easy terrain through the woods. The trail crosses a dirt road about a mile from the hike's start, passes over a small hill, and then crosses paved Westminster Road at 1.8 miles. After crossing a field, the trail enters the woods again, ascending a low hill and passing just below the summit. After crossing paved Administration Road, the Midstate Trail (here also called the Harrington Trail) reaches a junction with the Semuhenna Trail one mile from Westminster Road. The Semuhenna/Midstate turns left, but this hike continues straight up the Harrington another 0.3 mile to the Wachusett Mountain summit. Hike back the way you came.

Special note: To avoid backtracking, and for a somewhat shorter hike, shuttle vehicles to Wachusett Meadow and the Wachusett Mountain State Reservation Visitor Center and do this hike one-way. From the summit descend the Pine Hill Trail and Bicentennial Trail to the Wachusett Mountain Visitor Center, as described in the *Redemption Rock to Wachusett Mountain* listing in this chapter.

User Groups: Hikers only. This trail is not suitable for horses; no wheelchair facilities. Bikes and dogs are prohibited.

Permits: A fee of $4 per adult and $3 per child ages 3–12 and seniors is charged at Wachusett Meadow to nonmembers of the Massachusetts Audubon Society. A daily parking fee of $2 is collected mid-May–mid-October at Wachusett Mountain State Reservation.

Maps: A map of Wachusett Meadow is available at an information board beside the parking lot. A free contour map of hiking trails in the Wachusett Mountain State Reservation is available at the state reservation or at the Massachusetts Division of State Parks and Recreation website The Mount Wachusett and Leominster State Forest Trail Map costs $3.95 from New England Cartographics (413/549-4124 or toll-free 888/995-6277, www.necartographics.com). For a topographic area map, request Sterling from the USGS.

Directions: From the junction of Routes 62 and 31 in Princeton center, drive west on Route 62 for a half mile and turn right onto Goodnow Road at a sign for the Wachusett Meadow Sanctuary. Continue a mile to the end of the paved road and park at the sanctuary visitors center.

The Wachusett Meadow Visitor Center trails are open dawn–dusk Tuesday–Sunday and on Monday holidays. The Nature Center is open Tuesday–Saturday 10 A.M.–2 P.M. GPS Coordinates: 42.4521 N, 71.8922 W

Contact: Massachusetts Audubon Society Wachusett Meadow Wildlife Sanctuary, 113 Goodnow Rd., Princeton, MA 01541, 978/464-2712, wachusett@massaudubon. org. Massachusetts Division of State Parks and Recreation, 251 Causeway St., Suite 600, Boston, MA 02114-2104, 617/626-1250, www. state.ma.us/dem/forparks.htm.

🄹 MOUNT HOLYOKE
3.2 mi/2 hr 🏃3 ⛰8

in Skinner State Park in Hadley

Along the up-and-down ridge of 878-foot Mount Holyoke, the Summit House stands out prominently, easily visible to I-91 motorists several miles to the west. Although mostly wooded, the rugged Holyoke ridgeline has several overlooks that afford splendid views west to the Connecticut Valley and the Berkshires, and some views southward. This hike climbs about 700 feet in elevation, with much of the route along open ridge.

Follow the Metacomet-Monadnock Trail east from the road, immediately climbing a steep hillside; the trail soon swings north and ascends the ridge, reaching the first views in just over a half mile. At 1.6 miles, the trail passes by the historic Summit House, once a fashionable mountaintop hotel and now part of the state park; it's open weekends Memorial Day–Columbus Day for tours and programs. Picnic grounds also mark the top of Holyoke and numerous observation points offer unmatched views of the Connecticut Valley. You can return the way you came or continue over the summit, crossing the paved Mountain Road and turning right (south) in Taylor's Notch onto the red-blazed Dry Brook Trail. Follow it down the small valley, trending to the southwest and finally to the west and back to your vehicle.

User Groups: Hikers and leashed dogs. This trail is not suitable for bikes or horses; no wheelchair facilities.

Permits: Parking and access are free.

Maps: A free trail map of Skinner State Park is available at the Halfway House on Mountain Road (off Route 47) when a staff person is there; at the Notch Visitor Center on Route 116, where the Metacomet-Monadnock Trail crosses the road and enters Holyoke Range State Park in Amherst; or at the Massachusetts Division of State Parks and Recreation website. The Holyoke Range/Skinner State Park Trail Map (Western Section) costs $3.95 from New England Cartographics (413/549-4124 or toll-free 888/995-6277, www.necartographics.com). For a topographic area map, request Mount Holyoke from the USGS.

Directions: From the junction of Routes 47 and 9 in Hadley, drive south on Route 47 for 4.9 miles (you'll see the Summit House on the Mount Holyoke ridge straight ahead). Across from the Hockanum Cemetery, turn left, continue 0.1 mile, and park at the roadside where

the white blazes of the Metacomet-Monadnock Trail enter the woods on the right. Or from the junction of Routes 47 and 116 in South Hadley, drive north on Route 47 for 2.7 miles, turn right at Hockanum Cemetery, and then continue 0.1 mile to the trailhead.

GPS Coordinates: 42.3084 N, 72.5896 W

Contact: Skinner State Park, Rte. 47, Box 91, Hadley, MA 01035, 413/586-0350 or 413/253-2883. Massachusetts Division of State Parks and Recreation, 251 Causeway St., Suite 600, Boston, MA 02114-2104, 617/626-1250, www.state.ma.us/dem/forparks.htm.

15 RATTLESNAKE KNOB AND THE HORSE CAVES

4.5 mi/2.5 hr   🏃2 ⛰7

in Granby

The highest point on the saddle between Mounts Long and Norwottock, at an elevation of 813 feet, Rattlesnake Knob's relatively easy climb and excellent views make it a worthy destination along the ridgy Holyoke Range's eastern end. This hike also takes you to the Horse Caves, a large cleft in the rocks near the base of Mount Norwottuck. The caves are an interesting geological formation to explore, but are most well-known for the supposed role they played as the hideout for Daniel Shays and his followers after their raid on the Springfield Arsenal in 1786, part of the tax revolt known as Shay's Rebellion. This is a great hike for bringing history class alive for kids and only comes with a modest few hundred feet in elevation gain.

From the parking area, reach the trailhead at a brown metal gate marked Main Entrance. On the other side of the gate, follow the well-worn path to a junction at 0.2 mile. Here, bear right on the Upper Access Trail. For the next mile, the trail passes through a pleasant forest of oaks and hickory, stands of birch, and pine. Listen for the sound of woodpeckers and note their telltale drill holes in the bark of many of the trees along the route. At 0.9 mile, pass a rusted out old car (and make a guess as to how it ended up here) and then at 1.6 miles, bear right onto the red-blazed Cliffside Trail. From here it's only a few feet to a left turn onto the combined Robert Frost Trail (orange-blazed) and Metacomet-Monadnock Trail (white-blazed). At 1.7 miles, bear left again to stay with the orange and white blazes and begin to climb the rocky hillside. Reaching Rattlesnake Knob in another 0.1 mile, follow the sign marked To Viewpoint. From the open ledge of Rattlesnake, Mount Long rises in a green mound to the east and to the north lies the village of Amherst and surrounding Pioneer Valley countryside.

Backtracking from the viewing area, follow the orange and white blazes again as they pass over the knob and drop quickly to reach a sign for the Horse Caves (at 2.1 miles). Bear right and follow the Horse Cave trail less than a half mile to the caves; once you are done exploring, retrace your steps to the orange and white blazes and continue downhill. At the next junction, bear left onto the blue blazes of the Swamp Trail and follow 0.4 mile to a right turn onto the Southside Trail. At 3.2 miles, turn onto the trail marked Lower Access Trails to B-Street Gate. Follow past a large beaver dam and then bear right at the last trail junction before returning to your car.

User Groups: Hikers, dogs, bikes, and horses. No wheelchair facilities. The upper portions of this trail are unsuitable for bikes and horses.

Permits: Parking and access are free.

Maps: A free trail map and informational brochure are available at the park entrance at the Notch Visitor Center. For a topographic area map, request Holyoke from the USGS.

Directions: From Springfield, take I-91 north to Exit 19. From the exit, follow Route 9 east, soon crossing the Connecticut River. At 0.5 mile, turn right onto Bay Road, follow signs for Route 47 south. At 2.3 miles from the highway, turn left to remain on Bay Road and leave Route 47. At 5.2 miles, reach Atkins Farms Country Market and turn right onto

Route 116 south. At 6.4 miles, turn left into the Notch Visitor Center for free maps and an interesting natural history center. Reach the trailhead by continuing south on Route 116, turning left onto Amherst Street at 7.5 miles (at a sign for Route 202 and Granby). At 7.9 miles, turn left onto Bachelor Street. Finally, at 8.6 miles, park on either shoulder of the road when you reach a brown metal gate on your left.

GPS Coordinates: 42.2811 N, 72.4938 W

Contact: Mount Holyoke State Park, Rte. 116, Amherst, MA 01002, 413/586-0350. Massachusetts Division of State Parks and Recreation, 251 Causeway St., Suite 600, Boston, MA 02114-2104, 617/626-1250, www.state.ma.us/dem/forparks.htm.

16 QUABBIN RESERVOIR
4 mi/2 hr   🏃1 ⛰9

In Belchertown

Created in the 1930s by the construction of two huge earthen dams along the Swift River, the vast Quabbin Reservoir covers 39 square miles and is the main public water supply for the metro Boston area. Though artificial, the Quabbin still qualifies as the largest body of water in Massachusetts. Surrounding the reservoir is Quabbin Park, managed by the state as a recreational area, with hiking and bike trails crisscrossing acres of woods and many low, rolling hills. This easy hike takes you from Quabbin Hill to the scenic Enfield Lookout for expansive views of the reservoir and surrounding Swift River Valley.

From the parking area near the top of Quabbin Hill, walk a few more feet uphill to the stone observation tower and views north towards the water. Backtracking to the parking area, the yellow-blazed trailhead is located on the eastern end of the lot. Follow the trail on a gentle descent through pleasant woods; frequent breaks in the tress offer glimpses of the reservoir off in the distance. After a mile of walking, cross through a grassy area (follow the yellow markers) to a right turn onto a dirt jeep road. After only a few yards, arrive at an intersection with a paved road. Turn right on the paved road to reach the Enfield Lookout, an upland bluff not far from the shoreline and a popular perch for bird-watching—soaring bald eagles are frequently spotted here. To reach the water's edge, retrace your steps to the dirt road and take a right, descending another 0.75 mile through thick stands of pine (known as the Pine Plantation) before reaching the shore. For the two-mile return trip to your car, follow the dirt road back to the hiking trail, climbing uphill to the parking lot.

User Groups: Hikers only. Bikes are allowed on the dirt jeep road only (this can be picked up near the parking area). No dogs, horses, or wheelchair facilities.

Permits: Parking and access are free.

Maps: A free trail map is available at the Quabbin Visitor Center. For a topographic area map, request Holyoke from the USGS.

Directions: From the corner of West Street and Route 9/Main Street in downtown Ware, turn left on Main Street and follow for 4.7 miles to a right turn at a sign for the Quabbin Reservoir (as Route 9 leaves Ware, it is also called Belchertown Road). Follow the park access road for 0.3 mile to the parking area (almost at the top of Quabbin Hill).

State regulations require visitors to enter and exit through gates or other designated areas only; no off trail hiking or biking. Anything that could pollute the water supply system, such as litter or refuse of any sort, is prohibited. Direct water contact activities, such as swimming and wading, are strictly prohibited by regulation. Dogs, horses, and pets are not allowed on any property associated with Quabbin Reservoir.

GPS Coordinates: 42.2160 N, 71.9999 W

Contact: Quabbin Visitor Center, 485 Ware Rd. (Rte. 9), Belchertown, MA 01007, 413/323-7221. Massachusetts Division of State Parks and Recreation, 251 Causeway St., Suite 600, Boston, MA 02114-2104, 617/626-1250, www.state.ma.us/dem/forparks.htm.

⓱ SPENCER STATE FOREST
1 mi/0.5 hr　　　　🏃1 ⚠7

in Spencer

At almost 1,000 acres, Spencer State Forest is a landscape of hilly terrain, creeks, wetlands, and a beautiful transitional forest of oak, hickory, ash, and birch. The forest's most notable feature is the Howe Pond parcel, an estate formerly belonging to Elias Howe, the inventor of the sewing machine. Though the remains of the estate are limited to a mill pond and dam constructed by the inventor, their peaceful setting in the Spencer woods still makes for a pleasant, and relatively flat, forest ramble.

From the parking area, first take in the beauty of the woods by crossing the road and heading north along the old bridle trail. A loop of about a half mile, the trail takes you by the upper reaches of the Cranberry River, an especially pleasing stroll in autumn, when the wetlands here are a little less mosquito infested. Crossing over the river, the trail brings you back to the parking area. Next, head past the picnic area to reach the Howe Pond. The trail passes over the dam and then hugs the shore of the Mill Pond, a popular swimming hole in summer. There is no loop around the pond. Walk to the end of the trail about halfway around the water's edge, then turn around and walk back to your car.

User Groups: Hikers and leashed dogs. Bike and horses are allowed on the bridle path. Wheelchair users can get good views of the dam and pond from the wheelchair accessible picnic area.

Permits: Parking and access are free.

Maps: A free trail map is available near the picnic/parking area or online from the Massachusetts Division of State Parks and Recreation.

For a topographic area map, request Leicester from the USGS.

Directions: From the center of Spencer, head east on Main Street toward Maple Street. Take the first right onto Maple Street and follow for one mile to a right turn onto Howe Road. Follow Howe Road for one mile to the forest entrance; keep following the road a short distance to the parking and picnic area.

GPS Coordinates: 42.2158 N, 71.9990 W

Contact: Spencer State Forest, Howe Rd., Spencer, MA, 01562, 508/886-6333. Massachusetts Division of State Parks and Recreation, 251 Causeway St., Suite 600, Boston, MA 02114-2104, 617/626-1250, www.state.ma.us/dem/forparks.htm.

🔟 PURGATORY CHASM
0.5 mi/0.5 hr

in Purgatory Chasm State Reservation in Sutton

Short and sweet, this little adventure will have you scrambling over rocks and into the mouth of a chasm stretching a quarter mile before you, its floor littered with huge boulders. Rock walls rise as high as 70 feet on either side of this narrow defile, which geologists theorize was created by catastrophic force after melting glacial ice suddenly released torrents of flood water that shattered this gap through the granite bedrock. As if clinging to its prehistoric roots, Purgatory Chasm today is known to harbor pockets of ice into May and June. A nice escape on a hot summer day, the air is often at least 10 degrees cooler than in the parking lot you've just left behind. Although the scrambling can be difficult for people who are uncomfortable moving over rocks, this half-mile loop is mostly flat and a good one for children.

From the information kiosk, walk toward the pavilion, but before reaching it turn right where the blue-blazed Chasm Loop Trail leads down through the chasm; you may see rock climbers on the walls. At the chasm's far end, poke your head inside the aptly named Coffin, a tight space among the boulders to the trail's right. Then turn left and follow the Chasm Loop Trail's blue blazes uphill onto the rim above the chasm, past deep cracks that have been given such names as Fat Man's Misery and the Corn Crib. The trail leads back to the parking lot.

User Groups: Hikers and leashed dogs. No wheelchair facilities. The trail is not suitable for bikes, horses, or skis.

Permits: Parking and access are free.

Maps: A free map of hiking trails is available at the information kiosk and online from the Massachusetts Division of State Parks and Recreation. For topographic area maps, request Milford and Worcester South from the USGS.

Directions: From Route 146 in Northbridge, take the exit for Purgatory Road. Turn west on Purgatory Road and drive 0.6 mile to parking on the left, beside a pavilion and information kiosk. Purgatory Chasm State Reservation is open sunrise–sunset daily, year-round.

GPS Coordinates: 42.1260 N, 71.7010 W

Contact: Purgatory Chasm State Reservation, Purgatory Rd., Sutton, MA 01590, 508/234-3733. Massachusetts Division of State Parks and Recreation, 251 Causeway St., Suite 600, Boston, MA 02114-2104, 617/626-1250, www.state.ma.us/dem/forparks.htm.

🔟 CARPENTER ROCKS
2.5 mi/1.5 hr

in Wells State Park in Sturbridge

More than 10 miles of hiking trails crisscross this 1,400-acre woodland park, but the most popular route leads to the grand metamorphic cliff face at Carpenter Rocks. A low-elevation walk in the woods until a final scramble to the top of the cliffs, this trail also takes you to Mill Pond, a picturesque wetland that's a favorite hangout for local waterfowl.

From the parking area, follow the markers for the Mill Pond Trail. A little more than a quarter mile in length, this wheelchair accessible path hugs the shore of Mill Pond, a serene little pool of water that's home to ducks, Canada geese, and beaver. At the end of the trail, continue straight ahead onto the North Trail. In a very short distance, North Trail crosses a stream and reaches a trail junction. Here, turn left on the smaller footpath, this is the trail that will lead you to Carpenter Rocks. Continue on for another half mile through a mix of hardwood forest and wetland. As you come upon the cliff, the trail suddenly grows much more rugged and steep and, almost without knowing it, you are on the cliff tops taking in a sweeping vista of nearby Walker Pond and the surrounding wooded valley. Return the way you came.

User Groups: Hikers and leashed dogs. This hike is suitable for wheelchair users along the Mill Pond portion of the route. At the end of the Mill Pond Trail, wheelchair users can turn onto the park access road to return to the parking area. Bike and horses are allowed on certain park trails; the path to the Carpenter Rocks is for hikers and dogs only.

Permits: Parking and access are free.

Maps: A free trail map is available at the park entrance. For a topographic area map, request Southbridge from the USGS.

Directions: Follow the Massachusetts Turnpike (I-90) to Exit 9 (Sturbridge). After the toll booths, follow Route 20 east less than a mile to the intersection with Route 49. Turn left onto Route 49 North. The Park entrance is the third left off Route 49.

GPS Coordinates: 42.1425 N, 72.0408 W

Contact: Wells State Park, Rte. 49, Sturbridge, MA 01518 508/347-9257. Massachusetts Division of State Parks and Recreation, 251 Causeway St., Suite 600, Boston, MA 02114-2104, 617/626-1250, www.state.ma.us/dem/forparks.htm.

20 MIDSTATE TRAIL LOOP
6.5 mi/3.5 hr 　　　🥾5 ⛰7

in Douglas State Forest in Douglas

This loop, mostly on forest roads, uses the Midstate Trail to explore the big piece of Douglas State Forest that lies south of Route 16. The loop sections that employ forest roads are easy or moderately difficult for mountain bikers; however, the stretches that follow a rougher trail are more difficult. The Midstate Trail is fairly flat but crosses some streams and gets rocky in places. It's a well-blazed trail with yellow triangles, yet most other forest roads are not marked; use the map.

The Midstate Trail is accessed via the Coffeehouse Loop's southern arm, a forest road beginning at the south end of the parking lot. When you reach the Midstate Trail, turn right (north) onto it. The Midstate makes several turns and, three miles out, reaches a T intersection at a forest road; you'll probably hear traffic on Route 16 to the left. This loop turns right, following the forest road south. At a fork, bear right and cross the dirt Southwest Main Street (where, if you turned left, you would shortly reach the intersection of Cedar Road and Wallum Street). The next intersection reconnects you with the Midstate Trail; backtrack on the Midstate southbound to return.

User Groups: Hikers, bikers, leashed dogs, and horses. No wheelchair facilities.

Permits: A daily parking fee of $5 is collected mid-May–mid-October. The fee can be avoided by accessing the state forest at other roadside parking areas. Consult the map for other access points.

Maps: A free trail map and informational brochure are available at the park entrance or online from the Massachusetts Division of State Parks and Recreation. For a topographic area map, request Webster from the USGS.

Directions: From I-395, take Exit 2 for Route 16 east. Drive 5.1 miles and turn right onto Cedar Road (there may be no street sign) at the sign for Douglas State Forest. Drive 1.8 miles to a crossroads at Southwest Main Street and proceed straight through onto Wallum Street. At 0.9 mile farther, turn right into the state forest and drive 0.7 mile to an information panel where a box contains maps. Bear right and continue a short distance to a parking lot.

GPS Coordinates: 42.0413 N, 71.7627 W

Contact: Douglas State Forest, 107 Wallum Lake Rd., Douglas, MA 01516, 508/476-7872. Massachusetts Division of State Parks and Recreation, 251 Causeway St., Suite 600, Boston, MA 02114-2104, 617/626-1250, www.state.ma.us/dem/forparks.htm.

21 COFFEEHOUSE LOOP
2.2 mi/1.5 hr   🏃1 ⛰7

in Douglas State Forest in Douglas

This relatively flat trail makes a gentle loop through peaceful woods, with the terrain growing slightly rocky in only a few places. Easy to follow, with trail junctions clearly signed, this hike also offers access to a longer outing on the Midstate Trail for those with extra time and energy. The loop begins at the parking lot's north end, eventually reaches and coincides for a short distance with the Midstate Trail southbound, then diverges left from the Midstate Trail and returns to the parking lot via a forest road.

User Groups: Hikers, dogs, skiers, and snowshoers. Dogs must be leashed. No wheelchair facilities. Bikes and horses are prohibited on part of this loop. Hunting is allowed in season.

Permits: A daily parking fee of $5 is collected mid-May–mid-October. The fee can be avoided by accessing the state forest at other roadside parking areas. Consult the map for other access points.

Maps: A free trail map and informational brochure are available at the park entrance or online from the Massachusetts Division of State

Parks and Recreation. For a topographic area map, request Webster from the USGS.

Directions: From I-395, take Exit 2 for Route 16 east. Drive 5.1 miles and turn right onto Cedar Road (there may be no street sign) at the sign for Douglas State Forest. Drive 1.8 miles to a crossroads at Southwest Main Street and proceed straight through onto Wallum Street. At 0.9 mile farther, turn right into the state forest and drive 0.7 mile to an information panel where a box contains maps. Bear right and continue a short distance to a parking lot.

GPS Coordinates: 42.0413 N, 71.7627 W

Contact: Douglas State Forest, 107 Wallum Lake Rd., Douglas, MA 01516, 508/476-7872. Massachusetts Division of State Parks and Recreation, 251 Causeway St., Suite 600, Boston, MA 02114-2104, 617/626-1250, www.state.ma.us/dem/forparks.htm.

BOSTON AND CAPE COD

© JACQUELINE TOURVILLE

BEST HIKES

(Bird-Watching
Great Meadows National Wildlife Refuge, **page 88.**
Drumlin Farm Wildlife Sanctuary, **page 93.**
Caratunk Wildlife Refuge, **page 101.**

(Coastal or Island Hikes
Bar Head Drumlin/Plum Island, **page 83.**
World's End, **page 100.**
Province Lands Trail, **page 103.**
Great Island Trail, **page 103.**
Aquinnah, **page 107.**

(Kids
Minute Man National Historical Park, **page 91.**

(Sunrises
Bar Head Drumlin/Plum Island, **page 83.**

(Sunsets
Great Island Trail, **page 103.**
Aquinnah, **page 107.**

Even in the midst of New England's largest urban

area — and its premier natural tourist attraction — the landscape of eastern Massachusetts provides hikers with a surprisingly varied mix of trails. From the rocky and scenic Blue Hills and Middlesex Fells, two oases of quiet, wooded hills just minutes from downtown Boston, to such rare and cherished recreation areas as Walden Pond and the coastal dunes of the Cape Cod National Seashore, hikes in Greater Boston lead to unusual microenvironments, history-drenched waypoints, and much-needed breathing room from the urban hustle and bustle.

Trails closest to Boston occupy compact acreage, but elsewhere in the region, lands such as Bradley Palmer State Park and Myles Standish State Forest offer sprawling, four-season recreation centers for thousands of local residents. Likewise, the Trustees of Reservations properties — Noanet Woodlands, Rocky Woods, and World's End — provide valuable local places to walk, exercise, and sightsee. Maudslay State Park, Walden Pond State Park Reservation, and the Minuteman National Historical Park are not only great places to walk, but preserve invaluable pieces of local history. And Great Meadows, Plum Island, Caratunk, and Mass Audubon's Drumlin Farm Wildlife Sanctuary are on the must-see destinations list of many bird-watchers.

On the Cape Cod peninsula, the Cape Cod National Seashore occupies over forty miles of pristine sandy beach, marshes, ponds, and forested uplands. A true glimpse of Cape Cod's past and continuing ways of life, boardwalk covered trails lead through terrain with a windswept, still-wild feel. Highlights here include the Great Island Trail, an unforgettable place to watch the sunset over Cape Cod Bay, and the Province Lands Trail, taking you all the way to Race Point beach at the very tip of Cape Cod.

Winter weather is erratic in the Boston area, but generally milder in this area than much of New England, opening up opportunities for visiting many of these places year-round without having to deal with snow or extreme cold. More commonly, visitors must deal with wind and, in certain seasons, biting insects and traffic. Cape Cod sees more rain than snow in winter; if the weather is dry, and the winds calm, hiking here often extends into early December and starts again in early spring. No matter what time of year you take to the trails, your best bet is to dress in layers for changing conditions.

It's also a good idea to contact the land preserve or park you are visiting before setting out on your trip. Hiker regulations vary widely under different land-management agencies (including the National Parks Service and Massachusetts Audubon Society); be aware of pet restrictions and changing trail-use constraints.

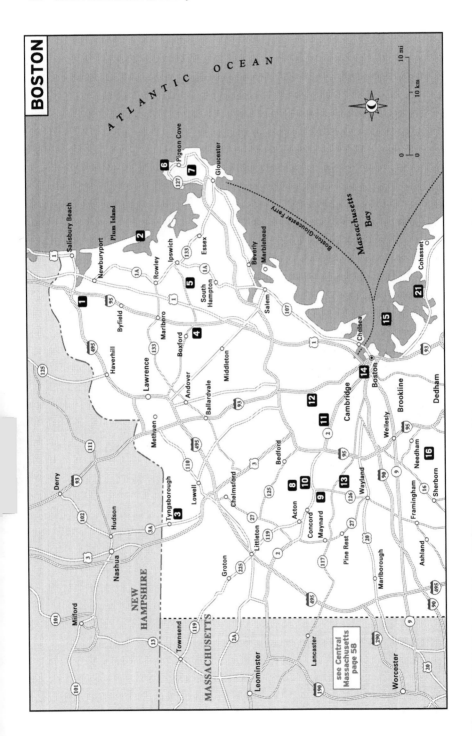

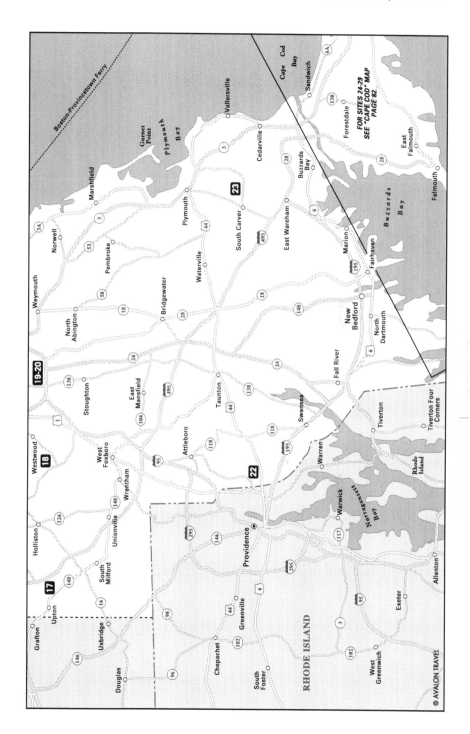

Boston-Provincetown Ferry

Cape Cod
Bay

FOR SITES 24-29
SEE "CAPE COD" MAP
PAGE 82

Sandwich
6A

Vallersville
138
Forestdale

East
Falmouth
28

Gurnet
Point

Plymouth
Bay

Marshfield
3
Cedarville
28

Buzzards
Bay

Falmouth

Norwell
3A
3

23

Plymouth

44

South Carver

Buzzards
Bay

Pembroke
53

495

East Wareham
6

Marion

Fairhaven
195

Weymouth
58

Waterville
18

Bridgewater
28

New
Bedford

North
Dartmouth
6

North
Abington
18

24

149

19-20

24

Fall River

138

East
Mansfield
495

Taunton
44

138

Swansea

118

195

Tiverton

Tiverton Four
Corners

Stoughton

104

1

Westwood
18

West
Foxboro
95

Attleboro

118

118

Warren

Rhode
Island

22

Wrentham
140

126

Unionville

146

Warwick
117

Holliston
South
Milford
140

17

Upton
16

95

Exeter

Allenton

Grafton
Uxbridge

295

Providence

146

6

295

117

3

98

Greenville
44

102

West
Greenwich
102

146
Douglas

96

Chepachet

South
Foster

RHODE ISLAND

Naragansett
Bay

© AVALON TRAVEL

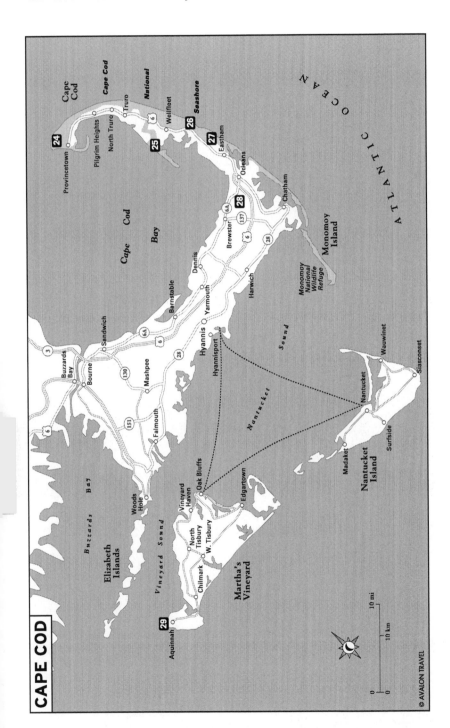

1 MAUDSLAY STATE PARK
2.5 mi/1.5 hr   🏃1 ▲8

in Newburyport

This 480-acre park on the Merrimack River was the 19th-century estate of the Moseleys, one of New England's wealthiest families. George Washington visited this area in 1789, and a regular ferry crossed the river here in the 17th century. Today you can hike trails through its many gardens and one of the largest naturally occurring mountain laurel stands in eastern Massachusetts, and stroll grounds where more flowers and plants bloom than you probably even knew existed. Mid-June is the time to catch the brilliant white flowers of the mountain laurel.

From the parking lot, walk past the headquarters to Curzon Mill Road, following it a short distance to a right turn onto Main Drive, a dirt road. Passing the beautiful Italian Gardens on the right and the pastoral Main House on the left, the trail ends at the Merrimack River Trail, which is marked by blue, white, and green blazes. Straight ahead is the Merrimack River. Turn right onto the Merrimack River Trail, following it along the hilltop and down into woods. After crossing two brooks on wooden bridges, the trail bears left onto another road and crosses over a dam at the end of the Flowering Pond. At the hike's halfway point, you reach the Laurel Walk, where the Merrimack River Trail branches right and left. The area to the left is closed November 1–March 31; take the right branch during these months. Otherwise, turn left and follow the Merrimack River Trail as it winds between the riverbank and the edge of the grove. Where the trail meets the Castle Hill Trail for the first time, bear left and stay with the Merrimack River Trail. Next, reach the end of a tree-lined road, another outlet of the Castle Hill Trail. Turn right to follow the Castle Hill Trail as it quickly crests Castle Hill, with views of the state park and this corner of the Merrimack Valley. Over the hilltop, turn right onto one road, quickly left onto another, and then right onto Line Road. It leads straight onto the Main Road (backtracking over the Merrimack River Trail's right branch). Take the stone bridge over the Flowering Pond, turn left onto the Pasture Trail, and follow it back to the parking lot. Picnickers are welcome.

User Groups: Hikers, bikers, leashed dogs, and horses. No wheelchair facilities.

Permits: A daily parking fee of $2 is collected year-round. A special-use permit is required for weddings, family reunions, and school groups.

Maps: A free, good trail map, including historical information and the seasons for viewing various park flora in bloom, is available at park headquarters. A basic map is also available at online from the Massachusetts Division of State Parks and Recreation website. For a topographic area map, request Newburyport from the USGS.

GPS Coordinates: 42.8224 N, 70.9218 W

Directions: From I-95, take Exit 57 in Newburyport for Route 113 west. Drive a half mile and then turn right onto Hoyt's Lane/Gypsy Lane. At the road's end, turn right (in front of the park headquarters) onto Pine Hill Road and right again into the parking lot. The park is open 8 A.M.–sunset year-round.

Contact: Maudslay State Park, Curzon's Mill Rd., Newburyport, MA 01950, 978/465-7223. Massachusetts Division of State Parks and Recreation, 251 Causeway St., Suite 600, Boston, MA 02114-2104, 617/626-1250, www.state.ma.us/dem/forparks.htm.

2 BAR HEAD DRUMLIN/ PLUM ISLAND
3 mi/1.5 hr   🏃2 ▲7

in Sandy Point State Reservation in Ipswich

BEST (

This easy hike combines a walk along a sandy beach and a rocky shoreline with a hike onto the glacial drumlin, an oval mound of earth deposited by a receding glacier 10,000 years ago. Today several plant and animal species rarely found near a sandy beach thrive on Bar Head Drumlin. Fifty feet high and covering 15 acres, the drumlin is shrinking under constant erosion by the ocean. Nearby, the sprawling Parker River National Wildlife Refuge is home to numerous bird species in summer, including cormorants, herons, kingfishers, and ducks. Nearly across from the parking area for this hike is an observation tower with a view of the refuge's marshlands. Bring bug repellent in summer—there are lots of biting insects, especially on the overgrown road along the refuge boundary. Inspect your skin and clothing afterward for ticks.

From the parking lot, pass through a gate onto the beach boardwalk and turn right. The trail—a rock-strewn stretch that eventually gives way to sandy beach—begins below the eroded cliffs of the Bar Head Drumlin. Follow the waterline around to the right until you reach a fence at the wildlife refuge boundary. Turn right and follow an overgrown road along the refuge boundary to a parking lot for the state reservation. Cross the lot to an unmarked, overgrown trail leading up onto Bar Head.

Although the trees and brush atop the drumlin are too dense and high to afford views, a few side trails to the cliffs permit beach and ocean views, good perches to watch the sun rise majestically over the open ocean waters. (Visiting in the early morning hours also helps you avoid the crowds that typically plague Bar Head in summer.) The trail leads over Bar Head and back to the beach near the boardwalk where you started.

User Groups: Hikers only. Bicycles are permitted only on the refuge road and in designated parking areas. No horses, dogs, or wheelchair facilities.

Permits: The fee for entering the Parker River National Wildlife Refuge is $5 per vehicle or $2 for anyone entering on foot or bike, year-round. During the warmer months, the refuge often fills to capacity and the entrance closes temporarily, even to visitors on foot. Arrive early to avoid this inconvenience.

Maps: No map is really needed for this hike, but two different maps are available at the refuge's website. For topographic area maps, request Ipswich and Newburyport from the USGS.

Directions: From I-95 take Exit 57 and travel east on Route 113, then continue straight onto U.S. 1A South to the intersection with Rolfe's Lane for a total of 3.5 miles. Turn left onto Rolfe's Lane and travel 0.5 mile to its end. Turn right onto the Plum Island Turnpike and travel two miles crossing the Sgt. Donald Wilkinson Bridge to Plum Island. Take your first right onto Sunset Drive and travel 0.5 mile to the refuge entrance. From the entrance, drive 6.5 miles to a dirt lot at the end of the road and park. Refuge headquarters is located at the north end of Plum Island near the Newburyport Harbor Lighthouse and is open Monday–Friday 8 A.M.–4:30 P.M., except on federal holidays.

The reservation is open daily sunrise–sunset. Walk only on trails, boardwalks, roads, parking areas, observation areas, and the beach; all other areas, including the dunes, are closed to the public. The beach is closed April 1 through at least July 1, portions possibly through late August, to protect nesting areas for the threatened piping plover. GPS Coordinates: 42.718 N, 70.7812 W
Contact: Parker River National Wildlife Refuge, 6 Plum Island Turnpike, Newburyport, MA 01950, 978/465-5753 or 800/877-8339 for the hearing impaired, http://parkerriver.fws.gov. U.S. Fish and Wildlife Service, 800/344-9453, www.fws.gov.

❸ LOWELL-DRACUT-TYNGSBORO STATE FOREST
2 mi/1 hr

In Tyngsboro and Lowell

Archaeologists believe the Lowell-Dracut-Tyngsboro State Forest, a collection of 1,140 acres dominated by ponds, swamps, wetlands, and mixed forest, was once the site of a precolonial Native American village. The backwoods oasis today stands in welcome contrast to busy city life, offering a kind of quiet and solitude that is often in short supply around these parts. The Family Loop Trail is a flat, easy loop that takes you into the heart of the Spruce Swamp, a marshy wetlands that is home to ducks, osprey, eagles, geese, owls, and even great blue heron.

From the parking area, pick up the marked Family Loop/Healthy Heart Trail. Following this loop clockwise, bear left. At first under heavy tree cover, the landscape opens up as the trail reaches the swamplands to views of marshy ponds, cattails, and jutting poles of deadened trees. Unique swamp-loving plant species are fun to spot here, including white water lily, yellowdock, and pickerel weed. Frogs leap and salamanders scamper off the trail, the call of ducks is constant, and mosquitoes buzz about in great quantity, especially in July and August. Finally reaching drier land, the loop dips back into the forest before returning to the parking area.

User Groups: Hikers and leashed dogs; no wheelchair facilities. This trail is not suitable for horses or bikes.

Permits: Parking and access are free.

Maps: A free map is available at the park entrance. The map can also be obtained online from the Massachusetts Division of State Parks and Recreation. For a topographic area map, request Nashua South from the USGS.

Directions: From the Drum Hill Rotary in Chelmsford, take the Drum Hill Road spoke. Follow the road, passing through five sets of lights and then crossing over the Merrimack River on the Rourk Bridge. Turn left at the lights on the other side of the bridge. In another 500 yards, turn right onto Old Ferry Road and then left onto Varnum Avenue. Follow for a half mile to a right turn onto Trotting Park Road. Parking lot is at the gate.

GPS Coordinates: 42.6498 N, 71.3708 W

Contact: Lowell-Dracut-Tyngsboro State Forest, Trotting Park Rd., Lowell, MA 01854, 978/369-6312. Massachusetts Division of State Parks and Recreation, 251 Causeway St., Suite 600, Boston, MA 02114-2104, 617/626-1250, www.state.ma.us/dem/forparks.htm.

4 BALD HILL
3 mi/2 hr

in Boxford State Forest

Here is yet another sizable chunk of state land on the North Shore with a wealth of trails ideal for many activities. This loop takes you through the forest's southeast corner and over Bald Hill, but there's a lot more to this place worth checking out. You may stumble across old gravestones or home foundations from when this was farmland. This loop largely follows forest roads, is hilly, and the terrain can be rocky and rugged—a challenge if you take to the trails on a mountain bike. Many trail intersections have numbered markers that correspond to numbers on the trail map. The forest tends toward the soggy, meaning a plague of mosquitoes in spring and early summer.

From the turnout, head past the gate onto the dirt Bald Hill Road. Past Crooked Pond, bear left at Intersection 14, and left again at Intersection 13. Farther along, turn right, climbing fairly steeply up Bald Hill. On its open summit, cross the field to the left and pick up a forest road heading back down. Bear right and you'll pass a stone foundation at the former Russell-Hooper farmhouse site (marked by a small sign). Just beyond it, to the right of the trail, is the Russell-Hooper barn site. Follow the trail around to the right. At Intersection 8A, turn right; eventually you follow white blazes. At Intersection 26, turn right again and follow this trail back to Intersection 13.

User Groups: Hikers, bikers, leashed dogs, and horses. No wheelchair facilities.

Permits: Parking and access are free.

Maps: A trail map is available online from the Massachusetts Division of State Parks and Recreation.

Directions: From I-95 in Boxford, take Exit 51 for Endicott Road. Drive west and turn right onto Middleton Road. After passing Fuller Lane on the right, continue on Middleton Road another 0.8 mile. Park at a roadside turnout on the left.

GPS Coordinates: 42.6475 N, 70.9990 W

Contact: Boxford State Forest, c/o Harold Parker State Forest, 1951 Turnpike Rd., North Andover, MA 01845-6326, 978/686-3391. Massachusetts Division of State Parks and Recreation, 251 Causeway St., Suite 600, Boston, MA 02114-2104, 617/626-1250, www.state.ma.us/dem/forparks.htm.

5 BRADLEY PALMER STATE PARK

2.5 mi/1.5 hr   👥2 ▲7

in Topsfield

Wild tansy grows along the trail in Bradley Palmer State Park.

One of Topsfield's more famous former residents, Bradley Palmer, was a noted attorney in the early 1900s who represented Sinclair Oil in the Teapot Dome Scandal and President Wilson at the Versailles Peace Conference after World War I. Palmer's 732-acre estate is now a multi-use recreation area marked by moderately sloping hills, wide forest roads, and rugged trails offering varied opportunities for mountain biking and hiking. This hike merely introduces you to this park; use it as a jumping off point for further exploration of this North Shore hidden gem.

From the parking area, cross the paved road and head onto a broad forest road. Bear left and start climbing Blueberry Hill (a rigorous climb on a bike). Take the third right onto another forest road and then the second left to reach the open hilltop. If you imagine entering the hilltop meadow at six o'clock, cross the hilltop and turn right, toward a road entering the woods at about three o'clock. Watch for a narrower trail exiting left off that road and follow it down a steep hill. Bear right onto another trail, which leads down to the Ipswich River and land in the Essex County Greenbelt. Turn left along a trail paralleling the river; you'll begin seeing the blue blazes, with a paw print on them, of the Discover Hamilton Trail. Where a footbridge leads right over the river, turn left up a forest road. At a long, wide meadow, turn right and continue onto a forest road back to the park headquarters.

User Groups: Hikers, bikers, leashed dogs, and horses. No wheelchair facilities.

Permits: A daily parking fee of $5 is collected mid-May–mid-October.

Maps: A free trail map is available at the park headquarters or online from the Massachusetts Division of State Parks and Recreation. For a topographic area map, request Georgetown from the USGS.

Directions: From U.S. 1 in Topsfield, turn east onto Ipswich Road (at a traffic light). Drive 1.2 miles and turn right onto Asbury Street.

© JACQUELINE TOURVILLE

The state park entrance is on the left, a short distance down the road. Park in a dirt area just before the state park headquarters.

GPS Coordinates: 42.6551 N, 70.9123 W

Contact: Bradley Palmer State Park, Asbury St., Topsfield, MA 01983, 978/887-5931. Massachusetts Division of State Parks and Recreation, 251 Causeway St., Suite 600, Boston, MA 02114-2104, 617/626-1250, www.state.ma.us/dem/forparks.htm.

6 HALIBUT POINT
0.5 mi/0.5 hr   🚶1 ⛺8

in Halibut Point State Park and Reservation in Rockport

Halibut Point consists of Halibut Point Reservation and Halibut Point State Park and is jointly managed by The Trustees of Reservations and the state. The state park surrounds the site of the former Babson Farm granite quarry, a small pond now filled with water and ringed by the sheer cliffs of the quarry walls. The park's name derives from "Haul About Point," the name given to the 50-foot granite cliff at the ocean's edge by sailors tacking around the point to approach Cape Ann.

From the parking lot, cross Gott Avenue, following signs to the park entrance. A short trail through trees leads to the quarry. The park headquarters is to the left. Take the trail that goes around the quarry to the right. You pass a mooring stone—an enormous granite slab sunk underwater that anchors an oak post used as a mooring for fishermen's boats. Turn onto a trail branching to the right, toward the ocean, to reach The Trustees of Reservations property. The shore here is very rocky, an extremely wild place when the surf is high; be sure not to get too close to the water because the riptide is powerful. Walk to the left along the shore and then follow a trail back up toward the quarry. To return, walk around the quarry to the left, which takes you back to the entrance trail.

User Groups: Hikers and leashed dogs. No wheelchair facilities. This trail is not suitable for bikes or horses.

Permits: No permits required. A $2 fee is charged for parking mid-May–mid-October. For the rest of the year, the park is open at no charge during the daylight hours. The Trustees of Reservations members park for free.

Maps: A free trail map is available at the park. A map is also available online from the Massachusetts Division of State Parks and Recreation.

Directions: From the junction of Routes 128 and 127, follow Route 127 north (on Eastern Avenue) toward Rockport. After three miles, turn left onto Railroad Avenue, which is still Route 127. After another 2.4 miles, turn right onto Gott Avenue. The parking lot is on the right a short distance up the road.

The park is open daily 8 A.M.–8 P.M. Memorial Day–Labor Day; a parking fee is charged. From Labor Day to Memorial Day the park is open sunrise–sunset.

GPS Coordinates: 42.6868 N, 70.6311 W

Contact: Halibut Point State Park, Gott Ave., Rockport, MA 01966, 978/546-2997. The Trustees of Reservations, Long Hill, 572 Essex St., Beverly, MA 01915-1530, 978/921-1944, www.thetrustees.org. Massachusetts Division of State Parks and Recreation, 251 Causeway St., Suite 600, Boston, MA 02114-2104, 617/626-1250, www.state.ma.us/dem/forparks.htm.

7 DOGTOWN
8.8 mi/4 hr   🚶3 ⛺7

in Gloucester and Rockport

This patch of untamed woods in the heart of Cape Ann has become a favorite among local hikers and mountain bikers for its rugged trails, glacial-erratic boulders scattered through the forest, and the legacy of a wealthy financier named Roger Babson. Earlier in this century, Babson hired stonecutters to carve sayings into rocks here like Get a Job and Never Try Never Win. The old woods roads along this hike carry names but are not maintained thoroughfares for motor vehicles; many are very difficult to negotiate, even for experienced mountain bikers. This rolling, nearly nine-mile route through Dogtown could take five hours hiking, three to four hours on bikes.

From the parking area, go around the gate and follow the rough dirt Dogtown Road for 1.2 miles, passing old cellar holes on the left, to Dogtown Square, a junction of trails where a rock is inscribed D.T. SQ. From Dogtown Square, turn right onto a rock-strewn dirt road and follow it for 0.1 mile, then turn right again (where the red blazes of the Beaver Dam Trail branch left) onto the Tent Rock Trail, sometimes called the Boulder Trail. It continues for a mile to Babson Reservoir, along the way passing the large boulders inscribed with messages such as Truth, Industry, and Help Mother. From the view of the reservoir, the trail turns left, crosses railroad tracks, and reaches the rough dirt Old Rockport Road behind Blackburn Industrial Park, 1.4 miles from Dogtown Square. Turn left and follow the road 1.2 miles to the Babson Museum on Eastern Avenue/Route 127. Behind the museum, turn left onto the red-blazed Beaver Dam Trail. Crossing the railroad tracks, then skipping back and forth across a brook, the trail passes over a small hill, takes a sharp right, and reaches Dogtown Square, 1.4 miles from the museum. Turn right onto Wharf Road and follow it 0.4 mile to Common Road. Turn right onto the Whale's Jaw Trail, pass a huge boulder called Peter's Pulpit at about 0.3 mile, and reach the Whale's Jaw, another massive boulder, at 0.8 mile. Backtrack the same way to Dogtown Square and follow Dogtown Road back to the parking area.

User Groups: Hikers, bikes, and dogs. No wheelchair facilities. This trail is not suitable for horses.

Permits: Parking and access are free.

Maps: A free trail map of Dogtown is available

from the Gloucester Chamber of Commerce. For a topographic area map, request Rockport from the USGS.

Directions: From the Grant Circle Rotary on Route 128 in Gloucester, take Route 127/Washington Street north for 0.9 mile and turn right onto Reynard Street. Follow Reynard Street to a left onto Cherry Street. Then turn right onto the access road to Dogtown, 1.5 miles from Grant Circle Rotary. Drive less than a half mile to a parking area and a gate.

GPS Coordinates: 42.6338 N, 70.6681 W

Contact: Cape Ann Chamber of Commerce, 33 Commercial St., Gloucester, MA 01930, 978/283-1601, www.capeannvacations.com.

8 GREAT MEADOWS NATIONAL WILDLIFE REFUGE

2 mi/1.5 hr   🏃1 ⛰9

in Concord

BEST (

Although most visitors here are bird-watchers, even the casual walker can't help but be impressed by the profusion of winged creatures on this 3,000-acre refuge, stretching along 12 miles of the Concord River. From great blue herons and osprey to songbirds and wood ducks, 221 bird species have been observed here. On this hike, binoculars are a must—the Dike Trail around the broad wetlands is considered one of the best birding sites in the state. Besides birds, animals such as deer, muskrats, foxes, raccoons, cottontail rabbits, and weasels call the refuge home. With all the standing water here, you can bet there are lots of bugs too, especially in spring. Interestingly, relics of human habitation here date back to 5500 B.C.

Before you begin your hike, check out the view from the observation tower beside the parking lot. Then pick up the Dike Trail, to the right of the tower, which traverses the meadows between Upper Pool and Lower

bird-watchers at Great Meadows National Wildlife Refuge

Pool. On the other side, the trail reaches the Concord River banks (where canoeists pull ashore to walk the trail). Turn left, following the trail along the Upper Pool about a quarter mile to the refuge boundary, marked by signs. Turn back and follow the trail around the Lower Pool. You can either double back or, where the Lower Pool ends, take the Edge Trail through the woods back to the entrance road. Turn right on the road to return to the parking lot.

Special note: You can canoe the gentle Sudbury and Concord Rivers through the refuge and put ashore here to walk this trail. Depending on how long a day trip you want, put in along either Route 27, Route 117, or Route 62 and take out along Route 225 on the Carlisle/Bedford line.

User Groups: Hikers, leashed dogs, and wheelchair users. No bikes or horses.

Permits: Parking and access are free.

Maps: A map of hiking trails and a number of brochures about Great Meadows, including a list of bird species sighted here, are available at the trailhead. For a topographic area map, request Maynard from the USGS.

Directions: From Main Street/Route 62 in Concord Center, drive 0.7 mile east towards Monument Square. Bear left onto Lowell Road at the square and then take a quick right onto Bedford Street, staying on Route 62. Follow Bedford Street for 1.3 miles, then turn left onto Monsen Road, a dead end street (You will see a small brown sign for Great Meadows just before the turn). Stay on Monsen Road until it ends in the Great Meadows parking area, next to the observation tower. GPS Coordinates: 42.4746 N, 71.3277 W

Contact: Great Meadows National Wildlife Refuge, Refuge Manager, 73 Weir Hill Rd., Sudbury, MA 01776, 978/443-4661, http://greatmeadows.fws.gov.

🟩 WALDEN POND

1.7 mi/1 hr

in Walden Pond State Park Reservation in Concord

In 1845, a 27-year-old former schoolteacher named Henry David Thoreau came to Walden

© JACQUELINE TOURVILLE

Walden Pond

Pond to live on 14 acres owned by his friend, Ralph Waldo Emerson. Thoreau built a small one-room cabin and began his "experiment in simplicity," living a sustenance lifestyle on the pond. At the time, much of Concord was already deforested and the land converted to farms, but the woods around Walden Pond had remained untouched because the sandy soil was not very fertile. Two years, two months, and two days later, Thoreau closed up his house and returned to village life in Concord. Emerson sold the cabin to his gardener. (The cabin no longer stands, but a replica can be seen beside the parking lot.) In 1854, Thoreau published *Walden, or Life in the Woods*, still considered a classic of American literature. Ever since, Walden Pond has stood as a symbol of the American conservation movement.

Today, Walden Pond sits in the middle of a small patch of woods within earshot of busy state routes and a railroad line, yet it remains popular with hikers and cross-country skiers, as well as anglers and canoeists (a boat launch is on the right side of Route 126, just beyond the parking area). Songbirds, Canada geese, and ducks are commonly seen here.

From the parking lot, cross Route 126 and walk downhill to the pond. From either end of the beach, the Pond Path circles the pond, usually staying just above the shoreline but offering almost constant pond views. It's a wide, mostly flat trail under the canopy of tall pines. A short side trail, marked by a sign along the Pond Path, leads to Thoreau's house site. Stay on the trails—erosion is a problem here.

User Groups: Hikers only. Wheelchair users can access the beginning of this trail above the beach on Walden Pond. Bikes, dogs, and horses are prohibited.

Permits: A daily parking fee of $5 is collected year-round.

Maps: A free map and an informational brochure about Walden Pond are available outside the Shop at Walden Pond, next to the park office at the parking lot's south end. The map can also be obtained online from the Massachusetts Division of State Parks and Recreation. For a topographic area map, request Maynard from the USGS.

Directions: From the junction of Routes 2 and 126 in Concord, drive south on Route 126 for

0.3 mile to the Walden Pond State Reservation entrance and parking lot on the left.

Park officials may close the entrance if the park reaches capacity. The park is open to the public 5 A.M.–sunset; check for the closing time posted in the parking lot.
GPS Coordinates: 42.4415 N, 71.3363 W
Contact: Walden Pond State Park Reservation, 915 Walden St./Rte. 126, Concord, MA 01742, 978/369-3254. Massachusetts Division of State Parks and Recreation, 251 Causeway St., Suite 600, Boston, MA 02114-2104, 617/626-1250, www.state.ma.us/dem/forparks.htm. The Shop at Walden Pond, 508/287-5477.

🔟 MINUTE MAN NATIONAL HISTORICAL PARK

11 mi/6 hr

in Concord

BEST (

Like an American history textbook come to life, this hike, retracing the route of the American Revolution's opening moments, is a Bay State gem and can't-miss national treasure. After the fateful "shot heard round the world" was fired on Lexington Green in the early morning hours of April 19, 1775, British soldiers continued their march to Concord on orders to seize a rebel cache of weapons. Turned back at North Bridge in Concord by farmers and villagers turned Minute Men soldiers overnight, British redcoats were unmercifully chased back to Boston by the rapidly growing ranks of rebel fighters. Much of the trail follows original remnants of the Battle Road; other sections leave the historic road to follow the route of the Minute Men, traversing the fields, wetlands, and forests that provided cover and the element of surprise for their guerrilla-style tactics. The flat, easy terrain and opportunity to bring history alive for kids makes this a great hike for families.

From the parking area at Meriam's Corner, the Battle Road begins near the Meriam House, site of the first rebel attacks on the Red Coats. Visit the house if you like, but the flat, wheelchair accessible path quickly veers into the adjacent farmland, notable as remaining in the same configuration as it was in 1775; it's easy to imagine the stealthily advancing Minute Men creeping across the freshly tilled earth. The trail then continues, passing historic homes of noted Patriot figures, preserved wayside taverns and inns, sites of intense fighting, and the Paul Revere capture site. Interpretative panels are frequent along the Battle Road path and original buildings still standing are open for visits during the summer tourist season. The path ends at Fisk Hill and the Ebenezer Fiske house site. Retrace your steps or loop back via a walking trail through historic pastureland.

Special Note: If an 11-mile round trip is not feasible, a walk to the Hartwell Tavern (at this hike's halfway point) creates a round-trip of about 5 history-rich miles. For even shorter walks to points along the trail, other parking areas off Lexington Road take you within steps of the Josiah Brooks House and Brooks Tavern (mile 1.5 of this hike), Hartwell Tavern (mile 2.5 of this hike), the Paul Revere capture site (mile 3.2 of this hike), and the Thomas Nelson House site (mile 4 of this hike).
User Groups: Hikers, leashed dogs, wheelchair hikers, and horses. Because the Battle Road Trail is primarily an educational trail, it is not suitable for high speed bicycling. If you do bring your bike, be aware that you will be sharing the trail with many others.
Permits: Parking and access are free.
Maps: A free map is available at Minute Man Visitor Center. For a topographic area map, request Concord from the USGS.
Directions: From Lexington, follow Route 2 west for approximately 6.5 miles to a right turn onto Bypass Road/Route 2A. At the end of the road, take a left onto Lexington Road. Follow brown signs for Minute Man National Historical Park/Meriam's Corner, taking a right about a half mile down the road into the

parking area for Meriam House. The Battle Road trail starts here.

GPS Coordinates: 42.4593 N, 71.3229 W

Contact: Minute Man Visitor Center, 250 North Great Rd., Lincoln MA, 01773, 978/369-6993, www.nps.gov/mima/index. htm.

11 MINUTEMAN BIKEWAY
11 mi/5.5 hr   👥1 🔺8

In Somerville, Cambridge, Arlington, Lexington, and Bedford

This paved bikeway follows a former railroad bed and is popular with walkers, runners, bicyclists, families, in-line skaters, and—when there's snow—cross-country skiers. Many people, particularly students, use the bikeway to commute to work and classes. The bikeway passes mainly through forest in Bedford and Lexington, and through a wetland in Lexington as well. From Arlington into Cambridge and Somerville, the bikeway becomes increasingly an urban recreation path. It is flat and can be done in sections of short lengths, which is why this receives an easy difficulty rating despite its 11-mile total length.

User Groups: Hikers, bikers, dogs, and wheelchair hikers. No horses.

Permits: Parking and access are free.

Maps: A brochure and map of the bikeway is available from the Arlington Planning Department. Boston's Bikemap, a detailed bicycling map of the metropolitan area, which includes the Minuteman Bikeway, is available for $4.25 from Rubel BikeMaps (P.O. Box 401035, Cambridge, MA 02140, www.bikemaps.com) and from area stores listed at the website. For topographic area maps, request Boston South, Boston North, and Maynard from the USGS.

Directions: The Minuteman Bikeway can be accessed from numerous points for walks or rides of virtually any distance. Its endpoints are behind the T station in Davis Square, between Holland Street and Meacham Road in Somerville; and at the junction of Railroad Avenue and Loomis Street in Bedford. Access points include Massachusetts Avenue in Cambridge at Cameron Avenue and Harvey Street, 0.4 mile south of Route 16; the Alewife T station at the junction of Routes 2 and 16; a parking lot on Lake Street in Arlington, just west of the Brooks Avenue traffic lights; Swan Place and Mystic Street in Arlington center, near the junction of Routes 2A and 60 (where the bikeway crosses Massachusetts Avenue); Park Avenue in Arlington (via a stairway), just north of Massachusetts Avenue; Maple Street (Route 2A) in Lexington; Woburn Street in Lexington, just west of Massachusetts Avenue; Hancock and Meriam Streets (at a large parking lot), off Bedford Street (Route 4 and Route 225) and the Lexington Battle Green; and Bedford Street (Route 4 and Route 225) between North Hancock and Revere Streets in Lexington.

GPS Coordinates to Bedford Trailhead: 42.4858 N, 71.2772 W

Contact: The Friends of the Minuteman Bikeway, www.minutemanbikeway.org. Rails to Trails Conservancy, 1100 17th St. Northwest, 10th floor, Washington, DC 20036, 202/331-9696, www.railtrails.org.

12 MIDDLESEX FELLS SKYLINE TRAIL
7 mi/4 hr   👥5 🔺8

In Middlesex Fells Reservation in Medford, Malden, Winchester, Melrose, and Stoneham

Even in the midst of some of Boston's busiest suburbs, you can still find quiet and solitude hiking the Fells, a 2,500-acre chunk of woods and hills located a few miles north of the city off I-93. ("Fells" is a Saxon word for rocky hills.) The Skyline Trail—the premier hiking circuit in the Fells—loops around the Winchester Reservoirs, passing through forest and traversing countless rocky ledges, some with good views of the surrounding hills and, occasionally, the Boston skyline. Perhaps the best view is from atop Pine Hill and the stone Wright's Tower lookout, near the start of this loop, which overlooks Boston's skyline and the Blue Hills to the south. The trail dries out fairly quickly after the snow melts—it's a glorious hike on the first warm day of spring. Bikes are prohibited from this trail, but there are many forest roads and trails forming a network through the Fells that offer good mountain biking opportunities.

From the parking lot, walk along the right side of Bellevue Pond and onto a wide forest road at the opposite end of the pond. Look for the white-blazed Skyline Trail leading to the right, up Pine Hill. The trail is generally easy to follow, but it crosses many other paths and forest roads, which can cause confusion; be sure to look for the white blazes. The loop eventually brings you back to this intersection.

User Groups: Hikers and leashed dogs. No wheelchair facilities or horses. Bikes are prohibited from the Skyline Trail. Mountain biking in groups of five or fewer is permitted on fire roads and the designated Mountain Bike Loop mid-April–mid-December. Mountain biking is not permitted on single-track (hiking) trails and is prohibited in all parts of the reservation January 1–April 15 to protect trails and fire roads from erosion damage during this often-muddy season.

Permits: Parking and access are free.

Maps: A trail map of the Middlesex Fells Reservation is available for $6 via mail (with SASE) from The Friends of Middlesex Fells Reservation. For a topographic map of area trails, request Boston North from the USGS.

Directions: Take I-93 to Exit 33 in Medford. From the traffic circle, turn onto South Border Road. Drive 0.2 mile and turn into a parking area on the right, at Bellevue Pond. The reservation is open year-round sunrise–sunset. GPS Coodinates: 42.4317 N, 71.1074 W

Contact: Middlesex Fells Reservation, 781/322-2851 or 781/662-5230. Massachusetts Division of Urban Parks and Recreation, Commissioner's Office, 20 Somerset

St., Boston, MA 02108, 617/722-5000, www.state.ma.us/mdc/mdc_home. The Friends of the Middlesex Fells Reservation, 4 Woodland Rd., Stoneham, MA 02180, 781/662-2340, www.fells.org.

13 DRUMLIN FARM WILDLIFE SANCTUARY
2 mi/1 hr   🏃1 ⛰7

in Lincoln

BEST (

A working farm and 232-acre Audubon sanctuary on the fringes of suburban Boston, Drumlin Farm maintains a variety of habitats for visitors to explore: grasslands, agricultural fields, shrubs and thickets, mature forests, and small ponds and swamps. This easy, ambling loop hike brings you to many of the farm's best features, including the sanctuary's namesake, a whale-shaped drumlin hill created long ago by glaciers and now one the highest points in the greater Boston area. On a clear day, views from the top offer glimpses of Mount Wachusett to the west and New Hampshire's Mount Monadnock almost due north.

From behind the Drumlin Farm Nature Center, pick up the Drumlin Loop at the trail marker. Bear left onto the loop, soon passing though mixed woods as the trail sweeps in a gentle curve to bring you to the top of the drumlin. Take in nice landscape views and be sure to look skyward: goshawks, red tail hawks, and turkey vultures are a common sight circling overhead. Continuing over the drumlin, pass the first junction with the Hayfield Loop Trail. A little farther, the trail reaches a split. To return almost immediately to the nature center, turn right to stay on the Drumlin Loop Trail (a completed loop of about just over a half mile). This hike, however, continues straight ahead on the marked Hayfield Loop Trail. Edging along fields, shrubs, thickets, and more trees, birds spotted in this area include field sparrows, yellow-bellied eastern meadowlarks, and indigo buntings. After passing a junction with the Town Trail, the Hayfield Loop sweeps left and soon reaches the Bobolink Trail. Turn left on the Bobolink Trail and skirt the dedicated bird conservation area. This is a good place to whip out the binoculars: More than 100 different species of birds call this area home. At the end of the Bobolink, turn left on the Field Trail and follow as it curves by fields and a sheep pasture and then passes a vernal pond. Now reaching the working farm itself, bear right to crest Bird Hill. At the bottom of the hill are the Farm Life Center and a variety of barns, stables, and farm animals awaiting your visit. From the Farm Life Center, bear right to return to the visitors center and parking area.

User Groups: Hikers only. No bikes, dogs, horses, or wheelchair facilities.

Permits: Admission is free for Massachusetts Audubon Society members. Nonmember adults, $6; nonmember children (ages 2–12) and seniors, $4.

Maps: A trail map is available at the visitors center. For a topographic map of area trails, request Concord from the USGS.

Directions: From Route 2 in Concord (east or west), turn onto Route 126 south (at the sign for Walden Pond, Framingham) and follow for 2.5 miles to the intersection of Route 126 and Route 117. Take a left onto Route 117 east and the sanctuary is one mile ahead on the right. GPS Coordinates: 42.4086 N, 71.3284 W

Contact: Massachusetts Audubon Society Drumlin Farm Wildlife Sanctuary, 208 South Great Rd., Lincoln, MA 01773, 781/259-2200, www.massaudubon.org.

14 CHARLES RIVER BIKE PATH: HARVARD UNIVERSITY

14 mi/6 hr   🚶1 ⛰8

In the Charles River Reservation, Boston, Cambridge, and Watertown

The paved Paul Dudley White Bike Path along both banks of the Charles River teems with activity weekday evenings and weekends: walkers, runners, in-line skaters, bicyclists, wheelchair users, skateboarders, people of all ages out getting exercise in the middle of the city. It is easily reached from such colleges as MIT, Boston University, and Harvard, and accesses such riverside attractions as the Esplanade and Hatch Shell, the sight of the famous Fourth of July Boston Pops Concert and fireworks. The bike path provides a more convenient, more pleasant, and often faster means of getting around the city than driving or using public transportation. Some sections of the path are quite wide, others no wider than a pair of bikes; likewise, some stretches see much heavier use than others. The entire path forms a 14-mile loop between the Museum of Science and Watertown Square and can be traveled in either direction and done in smaller sections, which is why this trail receives such an easy difficulty rating. The Cambridge side of the trail where it winds between the Charles River and Harvard University is arguably the most scenic stretch of the entire trail and the most recommendable for a walk.

From the end of Hawthorn Street, cross Memorial Drive and walk toward the river. Turn left (east) at the path, a paved strip running parallel to Memorial Drive and the river. As you walk, take in incomparable views across the river to Boston and, to the left, the historic red brick skyline of Harvard University. It's a leafy and shady walk thanks to lindens and maackias, as well as maples and stands of ancient oaks. Continue over JFK Street, passing the Harvard University Crew building. (Crew teams from both Harvard and Boston University can often be seen sculling the waters of the Charles.) Where Memorial Drive reaches an intersection with Flagg Street, you have reached the edge of the Harvard campus. Turn around and retrace your steps—this reverse vantage point is equal in its lovely Cambridge, Boston, and Charles River views. You can also cross the bridge and walk back along the Boston side of the river, but there the path is close to traffic and not as enjoyable.

User Groups: Hikers, bikers, leashed dogs, and wheelchair users. No horses.

Permits: Parking and access are free.

Maps: Boston's Bikemap, a detailed bicycling map of the metropolitan area, which covers the Paul Dudley White Charles River Bike Path, is available for $4.25 from Rubel BikeMaps (P.O. Box 401035, Cambridge, MA 02140, www.bikemaps.com) and from area stores listed at the website. For a topographic area map, request Boston South from the USGS.

Directions: The bike path runs for seven miles along both sides of the Charles River, from the Boston Museum of Science on the O'Brien Route/Route 28 to Watertown Square in Watertown (the junction of Routes 16 and 20), forming a 14-mile loop. It is accessible from numerous points in Boston, Cambridge, and Watertown, including the footbridges over Storrow Drive in Boston, although not from the Longfellow and Boston University bridges on the Boston side. For this portion of the bike path, leave your car in metered parking or one of the public parking lots near Harvard Square. From Harvard Square, follow Brattle Street to Hawthorn Street (a five-block walk). Turn left on Hawthorn Street and follow a few blocks to the intersection with Memorial Drive.

GPS Coordinates: 42.3762 N, 71.1200 W

Contact: Massachusetts Division of Urban Parks and Recreation, Commissioner's Office, 20 Somerset St., Boston, MA 02108, 617/722-5000, www.state.ma.us/mdc/mdc_home.

15 BOSTON HARBOR: SPECTACLE ISLAND AND GEORGES ISLAND

6 mi/3 hr   🏃1 ⏏8

In Boston Harbor

A bit of the rustic wild in full view of sleek, modern Boston, this fun hike—and quick and easy city escape—takes you on a day trip to Spectacle and Georges Islands, the two most popular destinations in the Boston Harbor island chain; both are maintained by the National Parks Service. Access to the islands is seasonal, with ferries running May–September. When planning for this trip, factor in a little more than an hour total for ferry boarding and the ride through Boston Harbor. How much time you spend exploring the islands is up to you (and the ferry schedule). Try leaving on an early morning ferry to give your trip a more leisurely pace.

Only a 10-minute boat ride from downtown Boston, tiny 105-acre Spectacle Island offers an incredible five miles of walking trails. From the ferry dock, wander out on the island's twisting footpaths. As you follow the windswept shore, turn inland to crest the island's 157 foot-high hill, with panoramic views of the harbor and the city. Tree cover here is sparse and there is really no way to get lost. (Low-lying cover is as much due to wind as it is to the island's once bleak past as a garbage dump for the city of Boston.) Spectacle's visitors center offers exhibits about island history and nature, restrooms, and a cafe; jazz concerts are held at the visitors center every Sunday afternoon in summer.

Twenty-five minutes from the hustle and bustle of Boston is Georges Island, a 39-acre pinpoint of land that manages to squeeze in a large dock, picnic grounds, open fields, paved walkways, a parade ground, gravel beach, and the remains of Fort Warren, a National Historic Landmark. Built in 1847, Fort Warren served as a training area, patrol point, and prison during the Civil War, gaining a favorable reputation for the humane treatment of its Confederate prisoners. National Park rangers offer guided tours of the fort several times each day during the summer (you can also explore on your own); on weekdays in the spring, the island is a popular destination for school field trips. For a little extra room to roam on what can be a very crowded piece of real estate, visit Georges Island at low tide. The island actually grows to 53 acres, perfect for a meandering stroll along the sandy shore.

User Groups: Hikers only. No bikes, dogs, or horses. The visitors center, beach, and portions of trail at Spectacle Island are wheelchair accessible. For wheelchair users and others interested in visiting Spectacle Island only, a separate ferry ticket is available.

Permits: Trail, beach, and Fort Warren access are free.

Maps: Maps of the islands are available at the Spectacle Island visitors center. For a topographic map of area trails, request Hull from the USGS.

Directions: Boston's Long Wharf is next to the Marriott Long Wharf hotel and across the street from Faneuil Hall Marketplace, a short walk from the MBTA's Blue Line/Aquarium stop and from both the Green and Orange Lines at Haymarket. Inexpensive parking is available at nearby Fan Pier.

Round-Trip ferry tickets from Boston to stops at Spectacle and Georges Islands are $14 for adults and $8 for children ages 3–11. Ferries depart Long Wharf for Georges and Spectacle Islands every hour on the hour 9 A.M.–4 P.M. Monday–Thursday, June 21–September 1. Return trips from Georges Island are every hour on the half-hour. On Fridays and weekends during the summer, ferries depart Long Wharf daily every half-hour 9 A.M.–5 P.M. Return trips from both Spectacle and Georges run hourly.

GPS Coordinates: 42.3601 N, 71.0496 W

Contact: Boston Harbor Islands Ferry, 408 Atlantic Ave., Boston, MA 02110, 617/223-8666, www.bostonislands.com. Boston Harbor Islands Partnership, 408 Atlantic Ave., Suite 228, Boston, MA 02110, 617/223-8666, www.nps.gov/boha/index.htm.

🔟 NOANET WOODLANDS
4 mi/2 hr   🏃3 ⛰️8

in Dover

The 695-acre Noanet Woodlands is a surprisingly quiet and secluded-feeling forest patch plunked down in the middle of suburbia. It might come as a shock to many first-time hikers of 387-foot Noanet Peak to find that virtually the only sign of civilization visible from this rocky knob is the Boston skyline 20 miles away, floating on the horizon like the Emerald City. You have to scan the unbroken forest and rolling hills for a glimpse of another building. And you may hear no other sounds than the breeze and singing of birds.

The yellow-blazed Caryl Trail begins at one end of the parking lot. Follow it to Junction 6 (trail junction signs are on trees) and turn left onto an unmarked trail. Pass a trail entering on the right. At the next junction, turn right and then left up a hill. You soon reach the open ledge atop Noanet Peak. After enjoying the view, walk to your right a short distance onto a trail that follows a wooded ridge crest, slowly descending to the Caryl Trail; turn left (you'll almost immediately recross the trail leading to Noanet's summit, but do not turn onto it). Follow the Caryl Trail to Junction 18 and walk straight onto the blue-blazed Peabody Trail. Pass ponds and the site of an old mill on the right. (From 1815 to 1840, Noanet Brook powered the Dover Union Iron Company. A flood breached the huge dam at Noanet Falls in 1876. In 1954, then-owner Amelia Peabody rebuilt the dam.) Bear left through Junction 4 and turn right onto the Caryl Trail again, which leads back to the parking lot.

User Groups: Hikers and horses. No wheelchair facilities. Bikes are allowed by permit only; the price of the permit is discounted for Trustees of Reservations members. Dogs are prohibited at Caryl Park, but visitors who walk to Noanet Woodlands can bring their dogs.

Permits: Parking and access are free. A biking permit can be obtained at the Noanet Woodlands ranger station at the Caryl Park entrance on weekends and holidays, or from the Southeast Region office of The Trustees of Reservations.

Maps: A trail map is posted on an information board at the trailhead, and one is available free from The Trustees of Reservations, either at the trailhead or through The Trustees headquarters. Major trail junctions in Noanet are marked with numbered signs that correspond to markings on the map. For topographic area maps, request Boston South, Framingham, Medfield, and Norwood from the USGS.

Directions: From I-95/Route 128, take Exit 17 onto Route 135 west. Drive about 0.6 mile and turn left at the traffic lights onto South Street. Drive 0.7 mile and bear left at a fork. After another 0.4 mile, turn left onto Chestnut Street. Cross the Charles River and enter Dover; turn right onto Dedham Street. Two miles past the river, turn left into Caryl Park; the sign is hard to see, but the parking lot is next to tennis courts. Noanet Woodlands is open to the public sunrise–sunset year-round.

GPS Coordinates: 42.2483 N, 71.2712 W

Contact: The Trustees of Reservations Southeast/Cape Cod Regional Office, The Bradley Estate, 2468B Washington St., Canton, MA 02021-1124, 781/821-2977, www.thetrustees. org.

17 WHISTLING CAVE
3 mi/1.5 hr

in Upton State Forest in Upton

Whistling Cave is not a cave but two large boulders, one leaning against the other, with a small passageway beneath them. It's located in an interesting little wooded stream valley littered with such boulders. Trails are well blazed, the forest road intersections are marked by signs, and the state forest has many more miles of both trails and roads. This hike has some hills but is relatively easy.

From the parking lot, head past the gate on a dirt forest road to the junction of Loop Road and Park Road. Bear right on Park Road, passing one blue-blazed trail on the left (which may not appear on the map). Continue up a gentle hill to a pullout on the left. The Whistling Cave Trail, marked by a sign and blazed with blue triangles, begins there. It soon drops over ledges and down a steep embankment, then levels out. You cross a couple of small brooks and then enter the area of boulders. Whistling Cave is right on the trail at this area's far end, shortly after you start up a hillside. Just beyond it, the trail ends at the junction of Middle Road and Loop Road. (To reach Whistling Cave on bikes, horses, or skis, take Loop Road to this intersection, walk or attempt to ski to the boulders, and double back.) You can return on either Loop Road or Middle Road; the former remains a forest road, while the latter eventually narrows to an easy trail marked by blue triangles.

User Groups: Hikers and leashed dogs. No bikes, horses, or wheelchair facilities.

Permits: Parking and access are free.

Maps: A free map is available at the state forest entrance or online from the Massachusetts Division of State Parks and Recreation. For a topographic area map, request Milford from the USGS.

Directions: From I-495, take Exit 21B for West Main Street, Upton, and drive 3.7 miles south to the junction of High Street, Hopkinton Road, and Westboro Road; there is a pond to the left. (The junction can be reached in the other direction from Route 140 in Upton center by taking North Main Street for a half mile.) Turn north onto Westboro Road, drive two miles, and then turn right at the sign for Upton State Forest. Bear right onto a dirt road and stop at the map box. Continue down that dirt road a short distance to a parking lot at a gate.

GPS Coordinates: 42.1971 N, 71.6107 W

Contact: Upton State Forest, 205 Westboro Rd., Upton, MA 01568, 508/278-6486. Massachusetts Division of State Parks and Recreation, 251 Causeway St., Suite 600, Boston, MA 02114-2104, 617/626-1250, www.state. ma.us/dem/forparks.htm.

18 ROCKY WOODS

2.3 mi/1.5 hr

in Medfield

This 491-acre patch of woodlands boasts more than 12 miles of cart paths and foot trails and is popular with locals for activities such as walking, cross-country skiing, and fishing (catch-and-release only). There are many more loop possibilities besides the one described here.

Walk down the entrance road to the Quarry Trail and follow it 0.1 mile along the shore of Chickering Pond. Bear left at Junction 2, continue 0.1 mile, and then continue straight through Junction 3. At Junction 4, a half mile from Junction 3, cross the Harwood Notch Trail diagonally, staying on the Quarry Trail. A quarter mile farther, at Junction 7, turn right on the Ridge Trail and walk 0.7 mile. Bear right at Junction 6, turn left immediately after that at Junction 5, and follow the cart path more than a half mile back to Junction 2. The pond and parking area lie straight ahead.

User Groups: Hikers, leashed dogs, bikes, and horses. No wheelchair facilities.

Permits: Admission is free for Trustees members. Nonmember adults $4; nonmember children (ages 12 and under) free. Fees collected by ranger on weekends and holidays; honor system applies at all other times.

Maps: A free trail map is available from the ranger on duty weekends and holidays. Trail intersections numbered on the map correspond to numbered trail signs. For topographic area maps, request Medfield and Norwood from the USGS.

Directions: From I-95/Route 128 in Westwood, take Exit 16B onto Route 109, driving west for 5.7 miles. Take a sharp right onto Hartford Street and continue 0.6 mile to the reservation entrance on the left. Or from the junction of Routes 27 and 109 in Medfield, drive 1.7 miles east on Route 109 and bear left on Hartford Street and park along that street. The reservation is open daily sunrise–sunset year-round.

GPS Coordinates: 42.2011 N, 71.2794 W

Contact: The Trustees of Reservations Southeast/Cape Cod Regional Office, The Bradley Estate, 2468B Washington St., Canton, MA 02021-1124, 781/821-2977, www.thetrustees.org.

19 BLUE HILLS: SKYLINE TRAIL LOOP

4.5 mi/2.5 hr

in the Blue Hills Reservation in Canton

With 5,800 forest acres spread over 20 hilltops, the Blue Hills Reservation in Quincy, Braintree, Randolph, Canton, and Milton comprises the largest tract of open space in Greater Boston. It hosts a broad diversity of flora and fauna, including the timber rattlesnake, which you are extremely unlikely to encounter given the snake's fear of people. The reservation harbors an extensive network of trails and carriage roads. But be aware that some are unmarked and confusing, and many are rocky and surprisingly rugged. At 635 feet, Great Blue Hill, near the reservation's western end, is the park's highest point and probably its most popular hike.

This 4.5-mile loop on the north and south branches of the Skyline Trail passes over Great Blue and four other hills, climbing a cumulative total of about 1,200 feet. It incorporates several good views—the best being the panorama from the stone tower on Great Blue, reached near this hike's end. In fact, while the native granite tower is less than 50 years old, it symbolizes this high point's long history. Patriots used Great Blue as a lookout during the Revolutionary War, lighting beacons up here to warn of any British attack. For several hundred years, fires have been lit on Great Blue to celebrate historic occurrences, beginning with the repeal of the Stamp Act and including the signing of the Declaration of Independence.

From the parking lot, walk back on Route 138 in the direction you came, watching for blue blazes that cross the road within 100 feet. Enter the woods at a granite post inscribed with the words Skyline Trail. The trail ascends steeply for a half mile, reaching open ledges and the carriage road just below the summit. Turn right on the carriage road, where blue blazes are often marked on stones. Pass the path leading to the summit (there aren't any views, and the weather observatory here is private property) and within 0.1 mile turn right with the blue blazes onto a footpath marked by a post inscribed South Skyline Trail. It descends ledges with good views of the Boston skyline and Houghton Pond, enters the woods, and, within a mile of Great Blue, reaches wooded Houghton Hill. Descend a short distance to Hillside Street, cross it, turn left, and follow the blue blazes about 150 feet to where the blazes direct you back across the street toward the reservation headquarters (passing a post marked North Skyline Trail). Walk up the driveway and left of the headquarters onto a carriage path. In about 75 feet, turn right at a sign onto the North Skyline Trail. In minutes you reach an open ledge on Hancock Hill with a view of Great Blue Hill.

Continuing over Hemenway Hill and Wolcott Hill in the next mile, watch for side paths leading right to views of Boston. The Skyline Trail drops downhill, crosses a carriage path, and then climbs the north side of Great Blue to the stone tower. Climb the stairs to the tower for a sweeping view of woods, city, and ocean. From the tower's observation deck looking west (out over the stone building beside the tower), you may see Mount Wachusett. Standing on the side of the tower facing Boston, look left: On a clear day, you'll spy Mount Monadnock between two tall radio towers in the distance. Descend the stone tower and turn right on the Skyline Trail, circling around Great Blue, past the posts marking the south and north Skyline Trail branches. Make a left turn at the third Skyline Trail post and descend a half mile to Route 138, where you began this hike.

User Groups: Hikers and leashed dogs. No wheelchair facilities. Bikes and horses are prohibited on this hike, but are permitted on some other specifically marked trails in the Blue Hills.

Permits: Parking and access are free.

Maps: A trail map of the Blue Hills is available at the reservation headquarters or the Massachusetts Audubon Society Blue Hills Trailside Museum. For a topographic area map, request Norwood from the USGS.

Directions: From I-93, take Exit 2B onto Route 138 north. Continue for nearly a half mile to a commuter parking lot on the left—park here for this hike. The Blue Hills Reservation Headquarters is located at 695 Hillside Street in Milton, 0.25 mile north of Houghton's Pond, beside the State Police Station. GPS Coordinates: 42.2141 N, 71.1200W

Contact: Blue Hills Reservation Headquarters, 695 Hillside St., Milton, MA 02186, 617/698-1802, www.mass.gov/dcr/parks/metroboston/blue.htm. Friends of the Blue Hills, P.O. Box 416, Milton, MA 02186, 781/828-1805, www.friendsofthebluehills.org. Massachusetts Audubon Society Blue Hills Trailside Museum, 1904 Canton Ave./Route 138, Milton, MA 02186, 781/333-0690, www.massaudubon.org/Nature_Connection/Sanctuaries/Blue_Hills.

20 BLUE HILLS: RATTLESNAKE AND WAMPATUCK HILLS
2.2 mi/1.5 hr   🏃2 ⛰8

in the Blue Hills Reservation in Braintree

While many hikers flock to the west side of the reservation and to Great Blue Hill, the east side of the reservation remains a fairly well-kept secret—and the views from there are arguably better than those from Great Blue Hill. Standing in a warm summer breeze on Rattlesnake Hill, gazing out over an expanse of woods to the Boston skyline in the distance, many who visit here are amazed to hear only the breeze and the singing of birds, despite having left the interstate behind just a half hour earlier and hiking merely a half mile.

From the roadside parking area, follow the Skyline Trail, which quickly ascends a short but steep hillside to a view of the thickly forested, rolling hills of the reservation and the Boston skyline beyond. The trail bends around an old quarry now filled with water, and about a half mile from the road reaches the rocky top of Rattlesnake Hill, with excellent views of the hills and skyline. Wampatuck Hill, with more good views, lies less than a half mile farther. There is a short, rocky scramble along the trail between Rattlesnake and Wampatuck that may be intimidating for some inexperienced hikers. Return the same way.

User Groups: Hikers and leashed dogs. No wheelchair facilities. Bikes and horses are prohibited on this hike, but are permitted on some other specifically marked trails in the Blue Hills.

Permits: Parking and access are free.

Maps: A trail map of the Blue Hills is available at the reservation headquarters or the Massachusetts Audubon Society Blue Hills Trailside Museum. For a topographic area map, request Norwood from the USGS.

Directions: From I-93 in Braintree, take Exit 6 and follow signs to Willard Street. About a mile from I-93, watch for the ice rink on the left. Drive 0.2 mile beyond the rink, turn left on Hayden Street, and then immediately left again on Wampatuck Road. Drive another 0.2 mile and park at the roadside on the right, where a post marks the Skyline Trail. The reservation headquarters is at 695 Hillside Street in Milton, reached via the reservation entrance on Route 138 or from Randolph Avenue (I-93 Exit 5). This trail is open dawn–8 P.M.
GPS Coordinates: 42.2368 N, 71.0321 W

Contact: Blue Hills Reservation Headquarters, 695 Hillside St., Milton, MA 02186, 617/698-1802, www.state.ma.us/mdc/blue.htm. Friends of the Blue Hills, P.O. Box 416, Milton, MA 02186, 781/828-1805, www. friendsofthebluehills.org. Massachusetts Audubon Society Blue Hills Trailside Museum, 1904 Canton Ave./Route 138, Milton, MA 02186, 781/333-0690, www.massaudubon.org/Nature_Connection/ Sanctuaries/ Blue_Hills.

21 WORLD'S END
2.9 mi/1.5 hr

in Hingham

BEST (

This 251-acre peninsula in Hingham nearly became a community of 163 homes in the late 1800s, when then-landowner John Brewer hired none other than the famous landscape architect Frederick Law Olmsted to design a landscape of carriage paths lined by English oaks and native hardwoods. That much was accomplished, but the Brewer family continued to farm the land rather than develop it. Today, thanks to The Trustees of Reservations, this string of four low hills rising above Hingham Harbor provides local people with a wonderful recreation area for walking, running, or cross-country skiing. Bird-watchers flock here, particularly in spring and fall, to observe migratory species. From various spots, you'll enjoy views of the Boston skyline, Hingham Harbor, and across the Weir River to Hull. This hike loops around the property's perimeter, but four miles of carriage paths and three miles of foot trails, all interconnected, offer many other possible routes for exploration.

From the entrance, walk straight (northwest) along the flat carriage path for a quarter mile and then bear left around the west flank of Planter's Hill. A quarter mile past Planter's, cross the narrow land bar between the harbor and river, and turn left onto another carriage road. This follows a half-mile curve around a hillside; turn left at the next junction of carriage paths. After another half mile, bear left again, reaching the land bar a quarter mile farther. Bear left, continue 0.3 mile, then turn right and walk nearly 0.4 mile back to the entrance.

User Groups: Hikers and leashed dogs. Horses are allowed by permit only from the Trustees of Reservations. No wheelchair facilities or bikes.

Permits: There is an entrance fee of $4.50 per person ages 12 and older, except for members of The Trustees of Reservations, who enter for free. Horse permits are free but must be obtained in advance by contacting the Trustees of Reservations Southeast/Cape Cod Regional Office.

Maps: A map of the carriage paths and trails is available free at the entrance. For a topographic area map, request Hull from the USGS.

Directions: From the junction of Routes 228 and 3A, drive north on Route 3A for 0.6 mile. Turn right on Summer Street, drive 0.3 mile, proceed straight through the traffic lights, and then continue another 0.8 mile to the World's End entrance. The reservation is open daily 8 A.M.–sunset year-round.

GPS Coordinates: 42.2480 N, 70.8727 W

Contact: The Trustees of Reservations Southeast/Cape Cod Regional Office, The Bradley Estate, 2468B Washington St., Canton, MA 02021-1124, 781/821-2977, www.thetrustees.org.

22 CARATUNK WILDLIFE REFUGE
2 mi/1 hr 🏃1 ⛰7

in Seekonk

BEST (

Bird-watchers will want to visit here during April and May or late August–October to catch the migratory birds, but this easy, two-mile walk mostly through woods is a satisfying outing any time of year. There are a few trail options in the refuge, all of them well blazed; this loop, mostly on the blue trail, is the longest, winding through much of the property, past open fields, wetlands, and two small ponds.

From the parking lot, walk to the right of the building, past the information kiosk

and along the field's right edge. Soon a short side path loops into the woods to the right, bringing you along a bog, then back out to the field. Walk a short distance farther along the field, then turn right onto the red trail. After passing through a pine grove and skirting the far edge of the same field where you began, turn right onto the yellow trail and then bear left onto the blue trail. At the edge of Muskrat Pond, turn right, staying on the blue trail past Ice Pond, crossing power lines, passing another pond, and continuing through the beech woods and a hemlock stand; you'll pass several trail junctions and loop back to the bog, where you begin backtracking on the blue trail. After crossing the power lines and passing Ice Pond in the other direction, stay on the blue trail past one junction with the yellow trail and then bear left onto the yellow trail at the next junction. Upon reaching the field, turn right on the red trail and follow it around the field back to the refuge office and parking lot.

User Groups: Hikers only. No bikes, dogs, horses, or wheelchair facilities.

Permits: A donation of $1 is requested for nonmembers of the Audubon Society.

Maps: A map is available at the refuge. For a topographic area map, request Providence from the USGS.

Directions: From I-95 in Attleboro, take Exit 2 onto Newport Avenue southbound/Route 1A. Drive 1.8 miles from the interstate, turn left onto Armistice Boulevard/Route 15, and follow it 1.2 miles to its end. Turn right onto Route 152 south, continue 0.6 mile, and then turn left at a church onto Brown Avenue. Proceed 0.8 mile farther to the refuge entrance on the right. The refuge is open daily sunrise–sunset. Visitors should stay on trails.

GPS Coordinates: 41.8743 N, 71.3179 W

Contact: Caratunk Wildlife Refuge, 301 Brown Ave., Seekonk, MA 02771, 508/761-8230. The Audubon Society of Rhode Island, 12 Sanderson Rd., Smithfield, RI 02917, 401/949-5454, www.asri.org.

23 MYLES STANDISH STATE FOREST LOOP

11 mi/6 hr   5 7

in Carver

Myles Standish State Forest sprawls over more than 14,000 acres, making it one of the largest public lands in Massachusetts. A grid work of old woods roads cuts through this pine barrens, along with a hiking trail and a paved bicycle path. This loop from the forest headquarters connects several dirt woods roads. The grid pattern of roads and the signs at many intersections makes navigating through this vast landscape easier than it might be otherwise, but bring a map. Although the pine-covered terrain is mostly flat, there are slight rises and dips that can make the workout a little harder if you take to the trail on a bike or cross-country skis.

From the parking lot, head back out onto Cranberry Road, turn right, and then immediately right again past the headquarters building onto paved Lower College Pond Road into the state forest. Within a half mile, bicyclists can turn left onto the paved bike path, which leads to the dirt Halfway Pond Road; others will continue a quarter mile on Lower College Pond Road to the Halfway Pond Road intersection. Turn left onto Halfway Pond Road, follow it a half mile to a crossroads, and turn right onto Jessup Road. Continue about 0.7 mile and bear right at a sign reading Ebeeme Road, which is shown as Jessup Road on the state map. A half mile farther, turn right at a crossroads onto Federal Pond Road. Follow it a mile, crossing the bridle trail, a gas line right-of-way, and Kamesit Way, and then turn right onto Sabbatia Road. Continue a mile and then turn left onto Three Cornered Pond Road. Reaching the paved Lower College Pond Road within a quarter mile, turn right, then bear left immediately and proceed straight onto the bridle path (don't turn left onto another bridle path branch),

marked by a horse symbol. In a quarter mile, at the next intersection, turn left onto Negas Road, continue a half mile, and then turn left onto paved Upper College Pond Road. Proceed nearly a half mile and turn right onto Three Cornered Pond Road. Three-quarters of a mile farther, turn right again onto Cobb Road and follow it 0.75 mile to its end. Turn right onto Halfway Pond Road, go about 0.2 mile, and then take the first left. In about 0.3 mile, turn left again onto Doctor's Pond Road, go a half mile, and then turn right onto Webster Springs Road. Follow it nearly a mile, crossing paved Circuit Drive, a dirt road, the bike path, and the bridle path before reaching Upper College Pond Road. Turn left, following the paved road nearly a half mile to its end. Turn right on paved Fearing Pond Road and continue a half mile back to the forest headquarters.

User Groups: Hikers, bikers, and leashed dogs. The paved bike path is wheelchair accessible. Horses are prohibited.

Permits: A daily parking fee of $5 is collected mid-May–mid-October.

Maps: A free, basic trail map of Myles Standish State Forest is available at the state forest headquarters or online from the Massachusetts Division of State Parks and Recreation. For topographic area maps, request Plymouth and Wareham from the USGS.

Directions: From I-495, take Exit 2 on the Middleborough-Wareham line onto Route 58 north. Drive 2.5 miles to where Route 58 turns left, but continue straight ahead, following signs for the state forest. Proceed another 0.8 mile, turn right onto Cranberry Road, and then drive 2.8 miles to the state forest headquarters and a parking lot on the left.

GPS Coordinates: 41.8389 N, 70.6941 W

Contact: Myles Standish State Forest, Cranberry Rd., P.O. Box 66, South Carver, MA 02366, 508/866-2526. Massachusetts Division of State Parks and Recreation, 251 Causeway St., Suite 600, Boston, MA 02114-2104, 617/626-1250, www.state.ma.us/dem/forparks.htm.

24 PROVINCE LANDS TRAIL
6 mi/3 hr   🚶1 ⛰8

in the Cape Cod National Seashore in Provincetown

BEST (

This paved path is popular with bikers, hikers, runners, in-line skaters, and others, and it's good for wheelchairs, too. Making a circuitous loop through forest, past ponds, and over sprawling sand dunes, this multi-use trail is the region's most geographically diverse. Be sure to take the spur path a half mile out to Race Point (included in the mileage), which is near the very tip of Massachusetts and a great place for whale-watching during the seasonal migrations, when the whales often swim close to shore. Heed the center dividing line on this path, especially around its many blind corners. Pick up the bike path from the Beech Forest parking lot; the loop returns here.

User Groups: Hikers, leashed dogs, bikes, and wheelchair users. Horses are prohibited.

Permits: Parking and access are free.

Maps: A guide to national seashore bike trails is available at the Province Lands and Salt Pond Visitor Centers in Eastham. The Cape Cod & North Shore Bicycle Map, a detailed map of roads and bike paths on Cape Cod and the Islands and Cape Ann and the North Shore, is available for $4.25 from Rubel BikeMaps (P.O. Box 401035, Cambridge, MA 02140, www.bikemaps.com) and from area stores listed at the website. Or get the waterproof Cape Cod National Seashore Map #250 for $11.95 from Trails Illustrated (800/962-1643, www.natgeomaps.com/ti_massachusetts.html). For a topographic area map, request Provincetown from the USGS.

Directions: Drive U.S. 6 east to Provincetown. At the traffic lights on U.S. 6, turn right onto Race Point Road. Continue to the Beech Forest parking area on the left; the Province Lands Visitor Center is a short distance farther on the right.

Trails are open to the public 6 A.M.– midnight. The Province Lands Visitor Center on Race Point Road is open daily 9 A.M.–4:30 P.M.

GPS Coordinates: 42.0600 N, 70.1906 W

Contact: Cape Cod National Seashore, 99 Marconi Station Site Rd., Wellfleet, MA 02667, 508/349-3785, www.nps.gov/caco/index.htm. Salt Pond Visitor Center (corner of Nauset Road and U.S. 6, Eastham), 508/255-3421. Province Lands Visitor Center (on Race Point Road, off U.S. 6, at the northern end of Cape Cod National Seashore and approximately one mile from Provincetown), 508/487-1256.

25 GREAT ISLAND TRAIL
6 mi/3.5 hr   🚶5 ⛰10

in the Cape Cod National Seashore in Wellfleet

BEST (

As the sinking sun ignites the dunes a vivid yellow, tiny crabs scatter in the growing shadows, and the shoreline takes on a bluish hue as the wet sand blends with the purple-indigo of Cape Cod Bay. This west-facing vantage point is simply the best place to take in the sunset on Cape Cod, both for the majestic views as well as the sense of solitude. Even in the middle of a crowded Cape Cod summer, come here towards dusk and your only company may be a lone sea kayaker paddling the glassy waters of the bay far offshore.

From the parking lot, the trail enters the woods, following a wide forest road. An optional side loop (adding two miles to the hike) leads to the Tavern Site, so named because fragments of a 17th-century tavern were excavated there; nothing remains today, however. The main trail leads over Great Beach Hill (which has no views) and out to the grasslands separating the beach from the forest. Follow that old road around to Jeremy Point overlook, where the dunes end abruptly and you reach the beach on Cape Cod Bay. At low tide, the long spit out to Jeremy Point may be walkable, but be aware that it disappears

© MARION GREEN

sunset over Cape Cod Bay

under the ocean when the tide rises. Return the way you came.

User Groups: Hikers only. No wheelchair facilities. Bikes, dogs, and horses are prohibited.

Permits: Parking and access are free.

Maps: An information board is at the trailhead, and trail information is available at the Salt Pond Visitor Center. The Cape Cod & North Shore Bicycle Map, a detailed map of roads and bike paths on Cape Cod and the Islands and Cape Ann and the North Shore, is available for $4.25 from Rubel BikeMaps (P.O. Box 401035, Cambridge, MA 02140, 617/776-6567, www.bikemaps.com) and from area stores listed at the website. Or get the waterproof Cape Cod National Seashore Map #250 for $11.95 from Trails Illustrated (800/962-1643, www.natgeomaps.com/

ti_massachusetts.html). For a topographic area map, request Wellfleet from the USGS.

Directions: From the Salt Pond Visitor Center at the Doane Road Exit in Eastham, drive U.S. 6 east for 8.2 miles. Turn left at the sign for Wellfleet Center and Harbor. Drive 0.4 mile and turn left at the sign for Blue Harbor. In another 0.6 mile you reach the marina; turn right, following the road (with the water on your left) for 2.5 miles to the Great Island parking lot on the left.

Trails are open to the public 6 A.M.–midnight. The Salt Pond Visitor Center is open daily 9 A.M.–4:30 P.M.

GPS Coordinates: 41.9351 N, 70.0682 W

Contact: Cape Cod National Seashore, 99 Marconi Station Site Rd., Wellfleet, MA 02667, 508/349-3785, www.nps.gov/caco/index.htm. Salt Pond Visitor Center (corner of Nauset Road and U.S. 6, Eastham), 508/255-3421. Province Lands Visitor Center, 508/487-1256.

26 ATLANTIC WHITE CEDAR SWAMP

1 mi/0.75 hr   🏃1 ⛰10

in the Cape Cod National Seashore in South Wellfleet

This is one of the true highlights of the national seashore, as much for the site's historic significance as for the short, but uniquely beautiful walk through a swamp. It was from this spot, on January 18, 1903, that the Italian Guglielmo Marconi transmitted the first two-way transoceanic communication and first wireless telegram between America and Europe. The four huge towers that once stood here are long gone; in fact, more than half the land where they stood has since eroded into the sea. Considering the way the ocean and wind continually batter this narrowest section of Cape Cod—the peninsula is barely a mile across here—one has to wonder how many years will elapse before the sea cuts the outer cape off completely from the mainland.

From the parking lot, the Atlantic White Cedar Swamp Trail begins among stunted oak and pine trees. But as you descend at a very gentle grade, the trees grow taller; they are more protected from the harsh ocean climate in this hollow of sorts. Pitch pine, black and white oak, golden beach-heather, and broom crowberry thrive here, though many are still twisted in the manner characteristic of a place buffeted by almost constant winds. The swamp itself is an eerie depression formed, like other kettles on the cape, by a melting glacial ice block. Crossing on a boardwalk, cedars crowd in from both sides, some leaning over it, creating an almost overwhelming sense of intimacy in this odd little forest. The trail emerges abruptly from the swamp onto an old sand road that leads back to the parking lot.

User Groups: Hikers only. The Marconi station is wheelchair accessible. Bikes, dogs, and horses are prohibited.

Permits: Parking and access are free.

Maps: A trail guide is available at the trailhead. Maps and information about the national seashore are available at the Salt Pond Visitor Center. The Cape Cod & North Shore Bicycle Map, a detailed map of roads and bike paths on Cape Cod and the Islands and Cape Ann and the North Shore, is available for $4.25 from Rubel BikeMaps (P.O. Box 401035, Cambridge, MA 02140, www.bikemaps.com) and from area stores listed at the website. Or get the waterproof Cape Cod National Seashore Map #250 for $11.95 from Trails Illustrated (800/962-1643, www.natgeomaps.com/ti_massachusetts.html). For a topographic area map, request Wellfleet from the USGS.

Directions: Drive U.S. 6 east to Eastham. Five miles beyond the Doane Road exit for the Salt Pond Visitor Center, turn right at signs for the Marconi station and continue to the parking lot. The Marconi station, which has historical displays, is between the lot and the beach. The trail begins at the parking lot.

Trails are open to the public 6 A.M.–

midnight. The Salt Pond Visitor Center is open daily 9 A.M.–4:30 P.M.

GPS Coordinates: 41.9044 N, 69.9843 W

Contact: Cape Cod National Seashore, 99 Marconi Station Site Rd., Wellfleet, MA 02667, 508/349-3785, www.nps.gov/caco/index.htm. Salt Pond Visitor Center (corner of Nauset Road and U.S. 6, Eastham), 508/255-3421. Province Lands Visitor Center, 508/487-1256.

27 NAUSET MARSH
1.2 mi/0.75 hr

in the Cape Cod National Seashore in Eastham

This easy-to-follow trail has numerous interpretive signs with information about its abundant flora and a good view of Nauset Marsh. From the visitors center parking lot, start out on the Buttonbush Trail for the Blind, which leads shortly to the Nauset Marsh Trail. The Marsh Trail passes through pitch pine, black cherry, and eastern red cedar trees, then follows the edge of Salt Pond. (The pond was created when a glacier receded and left behind enormous salt blocks, which eventually melted, leaving kettle ponds such as this one in their wake. The ocean later broke through a land barrier to infiltrate Salt Pond.) The trail then turns away from the channel connecting pond to ocean and enters a forest of honeysuckle and cedar. It passes an open overlook above Nauset Marsh, which at one time was navigable. After entering a forest of red cedar and bayberry, the trail passes a side path leading nearly a mile to a good view of the marsh at a spot marked by the Doane Memorial, a plaque paying tribute to a family that once owned land here. The loop culminates near the visitors center parking lot.

User Groups: Hikers only. The Buttonbush Trail for the Blind is wheelchair accessible; instead of taking a right onto the Nauset Marsh Trail, wheelchair users can stay on the Buttonbush for a scenic loop back to the visitors center. Bikes, dogs, and horses are prohibited.

Permits: Parking and access are free.

Maps: A trail guide is available in a box at the trailhead, and maps and information about the national seashore are available in the visitors center. The Cape Cod & North Shore Bicycle Map, a detailed map of roads and bike paths on Cape Cod and the Islands and Cape Ann and the North Shore, is available for $4.25 from Rubel BikeMaps (P.O. Box 401035, Cambridge, MA 02140, www.bikemaps.com) and from area stores listed at the website. Or get the waterproof Cape Cod National Seashore Map #250 for $11.95 from Trails Illustrated (800/962-1643, www.natgeomaps.com/ti_massachusetts.html). For a topographic area map, request Orleans from the USGS.

Directions: Drive U.S. 6 east to Eastham. Take the exit for Doane Road, following signs for national seashore information to the Salt Pond Visitor Center.

Trails are open to the public 6 A.M.–midnight. The Salt Pond Visitor Center is open daily 9 A.M.–4:30 P.M.

GPS Coordinates: 41.8404 N, 69.9616 W

Contact: Cape Cod National Seashore, 99 Marconi Station Site Rd., Wellfleet, MA 02667, 508/349-3785, www.nps.gov/caco/index.htm. Salt Pond Visitor Center (corner of Nauset Road and U.S. 6, Eastham), 508/255-3421. Province Lands Visitor Center, 508/487-1256.

▨ CAPE COD RAIL TRAIL
25 mi one-way/12 hr 🏃‍1 ▲7

in Dennis, Harwich, Brewster, Orleans, Eastham, and Wellfleet

Following a former railroad bed, the paved Cape Cod Rail Trail extends for 25 miles from Route 134 in South Dennis to Lecount Hollow Road in South Wellfleet, near the Cape Cod National Seashore's Marconi Visitor Center,

making for about a two-hour bike ride. The mostly flat, paved trail crosses cranberry bogs, forests, and several roads, providing numerous access and egress points, including at the entrance to Nickerson State Park on U.S. 6A in Brewster, and at Locust Road in Eastham, which is off U.S. 6 near the Cape Cod National Seashore's Salt Pond Visitor Center (Doane Road). The trail passes through Nickerson, which has its own hiking trail system and a bike path, and it connects with bike paths at the national seashore. The rail trail is very much a citizen's path—busy in the summer tourist months with cyclists, in-line skaters, walkers, wheelchair users, and adults and kids of all ages. You can do sections of varying length rather than the entire 25-mile distance, which is why this receives such an easy difficulty rating.

User Groups: Hikers, bikers, leashed dogs, horses, and wheelchair users.

Permits: Parking and access are free.

Maps: The Cape Cod & North Shore Bicycle Map, a detailed map of roads and bike paths on Cape Cod and the Islands and Cape Ann and the North Shore, is available for $4.25 from Rubel BikeMaps (P.O. Box 401035, Cambridge, MA 02140, www.bikemaps.com) and from area stores listed at the website. Or get the waterproof Cape Cod National Seashore Map #250 for $11.95 from Trails Illustrated (800/962-1643, www.natgeomaps.com/ti_massachusetts.html). For topographic area maps, request Dennis, Harwich, and Orleans from the USGS.

Directions: To reach the trail's western end, from U.S. 6 in Dennis, take Exit 9 onto Route 134 south. Proceed through two traffic signals to a large parking lot on the left for the Cape Cod Rail Trail. The eastern terminus is at Lecount Hollow Road in South Wellfleet, near the Cape Cod National Seashore's Marconi Visitor Center and off U.S. 6. The trail can be accessed at numerous points along its path.

GPS Coordinates: 41.9176 N, 69.9864 W

Contact: Cape Cod Rail Trail/Nickerson State Park, P.O. Box 787, Brewster, MA 02631,

the famous view of the lighthouse and cliffs at Aquinnah, Martha's Vineyard

508/896-3491, www.mass.gov/dcr/parks/ southeast/ccrt.htm. Massachusetts Division of Forests and Parks, 100 Cambridge St., 19th Floor, Boston, MA 02202, 800/831-0569 (in-state only) or 617/626-1250 ext. 1451. Rails to Trails Conservancy, 1100 17th St. NW, 10th floor, Washington, DC 20036, 202/331-9696, www.railtrails.org.

29 AQUINNAH
3 mi/1.5 hr   🏃🏃2 ⛰️9

in Aquinnah on Martha's Vineyard

BEST (

The vibrant pastels of the clay cliffs at Aquinnah, the westernmost point of Martha's Vineyard island, are an eye-catching attraction at any time of day, but particularly striking at sunset, when the sun's low, long rays bring out the layered browns, yellows, reds, whites, and deep grays. This hike is an easy walk along Moshup Beach and is popular with tourists. From the parking lot, follow the sandy trail, sometimes crossing a boardwalk, which parallels Moshup Road. Within minutes you are on the beach; turn right and follow the beach to the cliffs. At high tide, you may have difficulty walking to the far end of the cliffs. Head back the way you came.

User Groups: Hikers only. No dogs or wheelchair facilities. This trail is not suitable for bikes or horses.

Permits: A parking fee of $5 per hour or $15 maximum per day is charged Memorial Day weekend–mid-October, although cyclists, walkers, or anyone not parking a vehicle can access the beach for free.

Maps: Although no map is needed for this hike, for a topographic area map, request Squibnocket from the USGS.

Directions: The cliffs at Aquinnah are on Moshup Beach at the western tip of Martha's Vineyard, in the town of Aquinnah, and at the end of the State Road, which crosses the island from Vineyard Haven. Three seasonal ferry services make regular trips, May–October, to Vineyard Haven or Oak Bluffs from Falmouth (508/548-4800), and Hyannis on Cape Cod (508/778-2600), as well as from New Bedford, MA (508/997-1688). The Steamship Authority (508/477-8600) carries vehicles and passengers from Woods Hole on Cape Cod to Vineyard Haven year-round, and Woods Hole to Oak Bluffs May 15–October 15.

GPS Coordinates: 41.3877 N, 70.8348 W

Contact: Aquinnah Town Hall, 65 State Rd., Aquinnah, MA 02535, 508/645-2300. Martha's Vineyard Chamber of Commerce, P.O. Box 1698, Vineyard Haven, MA 02568, 508/693-0085, www.mvy.com/islandinfo/townAquinnah.html.

Index

www.moon.com

DESTINATIONS | ACTIVITIES | BLOGS | MAPS | BOOKS

MOON.COM is ready to help plan your next trip! Filled with fresh trip ideas and strategies, author interviews, informative travel blogs, a detailed map library, and descriptions of all the Moon guidebooks, Moon.com is all you need to get out and explore the world—or even places in your own backyard. While at Moon.com, sign up for our monthly e-newsletter for updates on new releases, travel tips, and expert advice from our on-the-go Moon authors. As always, when you travel with Moon, expect an experience that is uncommon and truly unique.

MOON IS ON FACEBOOK—BECOME A FAN!
JOIN THE MOON PHOTO GROUP ON FLICKR

MOON OUTDOORS

"Well written, thoroughly researched, and packed full of useful information and advice, these guides really do get you into the outdoors."

—GORP.COM

ALSO AVAILABLE AS FOGHORN OUTDOORS ACTIVITY GUIDES:

250 Great Hikes in
   California's National Parks
California Golf
California Waterfalls
California Wildlife
Camper's Companion
Easy Biking in Northern
   California
Easy Hiking in Northern
   California

Easy Hiking in Southern
   California
Georgia & Alabama Camping
Maine Hiking
Massachusetts Hiking
New England Cabins
   & Cottages
New England Camping

New Hampshire Hiking
Southern California
   Cabins & Cottages
Tom Stienstra's Bay Area
   Recreation
Vermont Hiking
Washington Boating
   & Water Sports

MOON MASSACHUSETTS HIKING

Avalon Travel
a member of the Perseus Books Group
1700 Fourth Street
Berkeley, CA 94710, USA
www.moon.com

Editor: Elizabeth Hollis Hansen
Series Manager: Sabrina Young
Copy Editor: Naomi Adler Dancis
Graphics and Production Coordinator:
   Domini Dragoone
Cover Designer: Domini Dragoone
Interior Designer: Darren Alessi
Map Editor: Mike Morgenfeld
Cartographers: Mike Morgenfeld, Kat Bennett
Proofreader: Nikki Ioakimedes

ISBN-13: 978-1-59880-565-9

Text © 2010 by Avalon Travel and Jacqueline Tourville.
Maps © 2010 by Avalon Travel.
All rights reserved.

Front cover photo: Springtime water flow in the Quabinn wilderness in Massachusetts © Denis Jr. Tangney/istockphoto.com
Title page photo: Bash Bish Falls © Jaroslaw Trapszo

Printed in the United States of America

ABOUT THE AUTHOR

Jacqueline Tourville

Jacqueline Tourville grew up hiking in the Adirondacks region of New York State. As an adult, she discovered the diverse terrain of New England while living in Boston. Today, she's a busy freelance writer and author of the popular "Are We There Yet?" family travel column for *Parenting New Hampshire* magazine. She is the co-author of the prenatal health guide *Big, Beautiful and Pregnant,* and has contributed numerous articles about health and outdoor living for both web and print publications. Jacqueline lives in New Hampshire with her husband and two children.

Made in the USA
Lexington, KY
17 April 2013